Plastic Canvaswork

21 QUICK & EASY PROJECTS
FOR THE HOME

MEG EVANS

Plastic Canvaswork

MEG EVANS

ANAYA, COLLINS & BROWN
LONDON

DEDICATION
For my three lovely granddaughters, Penny, Ruth and Claudia.

First published in Great Britain in 1995 by Anaya, Collins & Brown Limited,
London House, Great Eastern Wharf, Parkgate Road, London SW11 4NQ

Editor   Felicity Jackson
Design   Watermark Communications Group Ltd
Photographer   Shona Wood
Chart Illustrator   Anthony Duke
Illustrator   Terry Evans

British Library Cataloguing in Publication Data:
A catalogue record for this book is available from the British Library

ISBN 1-85470-222-X

Colour reproduction by J. Film, Singapore
Printed and bound by Graficas Reunidas, Spain

Contents

Introduction

Plastic canvas has been available for embroidery for over a decade. At first it was mainly used for simple items, but as ideas developed it has become a medium for constructing a wide range of 3-dimensional projects which would be far more difficult, or perhaps impossible, to make using traditional materials.

Because the canvas is rigid, it will not go out of shape during handling, and working on a frame is not necessary. It does not fray, so turnings are not needed, and the pieces are embroidered and stitched together with the minimum amount of effort. It is washable, and if the correct yarns are used, it is hard-wearing, though probably not as long lasting as cotton or linen canvas. It is very much quicker to work on.

The fact that it is rigid means that it is not suitable for items which need to be soft or ones you want to drape. Natural fabrics are the best choice for these.

Personally, I like to use my embroidery. I have many of my embroidered panels on the walls, but there is a limit to the amount of space available, so it is very rewarding to make things which can be used for utilitarian purposes and, at the same time, add colour to one's daily life.

Bathrooms, for example, tend to be mainly smooth and rather shiny. Pretty embroidered boxes and containers can add some very welcome texture, and, if the colours are carefully chosen, can also add a touch of elegance. Co-ordinating accessories help to give a room a really cared for appearance.

The easy care properties of embroidery on plastic canvas ensure that they can be kept looking new during use. The ideas in this book are just a beginning: the same designs could be adapted for other items, a spare toilet roll holder and a rug in the bathroom, bedside tablemats and a cosmetic tray in the bedroom, and so on in each room.

Embroidered gifts are a very special way of welcoming a new baby. A growing child would be very proud of its own special 'picture' or the bag featured on page 54, which can be used for all sorts of treasures when the initial purpose is outgrown. The recommended yarns are both washable and hard wearing. If these are varied, make sure that the ones you choose have the same qualities.

Festive hand-made items, which are brought out annually at Christmas, give pleasure to the whole family, and the ones in this book will be treasured from year to year. A variety of yarns have been used, such as lustrous ribbon contrasting with the chunky double cross stitch in the table runner. As plastic canvas is quick to work on, experimenting with new colours and patterns is not the arduous task it is on a finer fabric. It is fun to adapt one pattern for another use. The pattern for the top of the playing cards box on page 31 is worked on 10 count canvas, and 7 count canvas has been used for the waste paper bin. The same pattern is adapted to suit the tall nature of the bin, the main motif being turned on end and the leaves moved in to meet at the centre. In the plant pot holder, the centre of the motif only is used, the colours being reversed here to give a dark flower on a light background.

The use of ribbon combined with the sheen of pearl cotton gives the bedroom accessories a rich, lustrous appearance. Ribbon needs a little extra care when stitching as the twist needs to be removed with every stitch, but the lovely texture achieved amply repays the effort.

Changing the colours and yarns used can produce quite a different effect even with the same pattern. The dressing table set for the bedroom, for instance, could be made in dramatic dark colours instead of the pastel shades used here. Whatever you do, keep in mind the room in which the item is likely to be used, and choose the various colours accordingly.

Bedroom and Bathroom

Boutique tissue box cover • Jewellery box
Basket • Picture frame • Manicure box

Boutique tissue box cover

This tissue box cover fits a 4½ x 4 x 5in (11.5 x 10 x 12.5cm) box of tissues, but adjustments are given for the larger size, which is 4½in (11.5cm) square, 5½in (14cm) deep.

Materials

Plastic canvas 7 bars per 1in (2.5cm): one sheet 13½ x 10½in (34.5 x 26.5cm)
Offray ribbon 3mm wide: 26yds (24m) 815 cream
Anchor No. 5 pearl cotton, 5gm skeins: five 75 pink and one 214 green

Preparation

1 For the smaller box, cut the plastic canvas to give two sides 34 x 30 bars, two sides 34 x 26 bars and one top 30 x 26 bars. Do not cut the hole in the top until the embroidery is completed. For the larger box, cut four sides 30 x 36 bars and one top 30 bars square.

2 Mark the centre line of holes in both directions with a line of tacking (basting) stitches.

Working the embroidery

3 Work in satin stitch blocks and lines, using ribbon or 3 thicknesses of pearl cotton. For the larger sides, follow the bottom chart on the right and work 2 pieces (4 pieces for the larger box).

4 Work a line of tent stitch in pink pearl all round. (If making the larger size, work an extra row of tent stitch across the top and base edges.) Inside this, work a line of satin stitch across the top and the base. Work the ribbon embroidery. Each quarter will need 49in

(1.25m) in the needle. Fill in the pearl cotton in green and pink.

5 For the smaller sides, work 2 pieces following the top chart on the right (this is for the smaller size only).

6 For the top, follow the middle chart on the right for the smaller size. For the larger size, the pattern will be symmetrical.

Finishing

7 Use pink pearl doubled for sewing up the box. Very carefully cut out the central uncovered area of the top, taking care to leave one bar beside the embroidery. Edge stitch all the way round.

8 Place one side against the top, right sides outside, uncovered edges matched up, and edge stitch to join them. Repeat with the other 3 sides. Edge stitch the corners to join them. Edge stitch all round the lower edge to complete the cover.

KEY

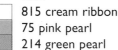
815 cream ribbon
75 pink pearl
214 green pearl

Smaller sides

Top

Large sides

Jewellery box

This is the simplest kind of box with a hinged lid and tassel for opening. The satin stitches at the centre of the design could be padded to make them slightly raised, if wished.

Materials

Plastic canvas 7 bars per 1in (2.5cm): one sheet of ultra stiff 18 x 12in (46 x 30cm) (This gives sufficient canvas to make the picture frame too)

Offray ribbon, 3mm wide: 15⅜yds (14m) 815 cream

Anchor No. 5 pearl cotton, 5gm skeins: four 75 pink

Lining: lightweight cotton or polycotton 32 x 5½in (80 x 14cm)

Terylene wadding: 18 x 5in (46 x 12.5cm)

2mm card: one piece 18 x 4½in (46 x 11.5cm)

1mm card: one piece 4in (10cm) square

Latex or clear adhesive

Preparation

1 Cut the canvas to give a base and a top each 28 bars square, and four sides 28 x 14 bars. Mark the centre line of holes on each piece with a line of tacking (basting) stitches in both directions.

Working the embroidery

2 Work in satin stitch blocks and lines, using ribbon or 3 thicknesses of pearl cotton. For the lid, working from the charts, first work the 4 satin stitch blocks at the centre of the top section. Then complete the cream ribbon embroidery, followed by the pink pearl.

3 For the box sides, work the ribbon embroidery, followed by the pink pearl.

4 For the base of the box, follow the pattern for the lid, or, if preferred, work a name and date instead of the pattern.

Finishing

5 Place one of the sides against the base, right sides outside and uncovered edges matched up, and edge stitch to join. Repeat for the other 3 sides. Edge stitch the corners to join. Edge stitch round 3 sides of the top and round 3 sides of the lid.

6 Cut the 2mm card to give two pieces 4 x 1⅞in (10 x 4.8cm), two pieces 3¹³⁄₁₆ x 1⅞in (9.7 x 4.8cm) and two pieces 3¹³⁄₁₆in (9.7cm) square. Using the card as a guide, cut out the lining fabric as shown in the diagram, allowing at least ⅜in (2cm) turnings all round. Using the 2mm card as a guide, cut the terylene wadding for the 4 sides, the base and the lid. The thinner card for the lid is not padded like the other pieces.

7 Place one of the pieces of fabric for the lid right side down and place the thin card centrally over it. Trim the corners and turn over and stick the turnings to the wrong side.

8 Place the second piece of fabric for the lid right side down, with the wadding for the lid centrally over it, followed by the 2mm card. Trim the corners and fold the turnings to the wrong side and stick in place. Cover the pieces of card for the base and the 4 sides of the box in the same way.

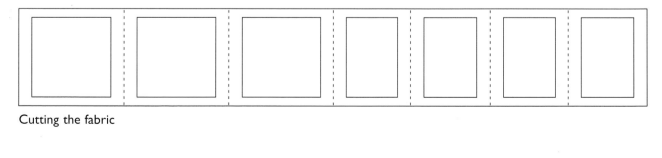

Cutting the fabric

Cutting the wadding

Top

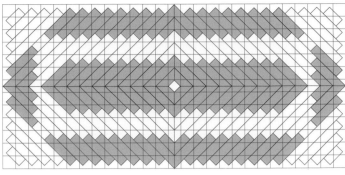

Sides

KEY

☐ 815 cream ribbon
▨ 75 pink pearl

9 Stick or slip stitch the thinner piece of prepared card centrally to the wrong side of the embroidered lid. Stick the thicker smaller piece centrally over it. Place a weight on top until bonded.

10 Spread adhesive along the edges of the longer side lining pieces and place them inside the box, using clothes pegs or similar to hold until bonded. Repeat with the shorter sides. These fit between the first two, giving the box rigidity. Slip the covered base into place.

11 Place the lid in position over the box, uncovered edges matching, and edge stitch through both layers to join. Do not work at tight tension as this will prevent the lid from closing properly.

Making a tassel

12 Wind some pink pearl cotton round 3 fingers about 15 times. Slip the loops off. Cut a length of pearl cotton, about 18in (46cm) long, double it and slip the folded end through the tassel. Take the ends through the loop and pull tight.

13 Thread both ends into a tapestry needle and stitch to the centre of the opening side of the lid. Wrap the thread around the tassel, about ¼in (6mm) down, and make a knot or two in it to secure the head of the tassel.

14 Take the ends down through the centre of the tassel and let them join the loop. Cut the loop and trim the ends to a suitable length.

Embroidering with ribbon

The ribbon should be flat, especially on the right side. As you work each stitch, hold it between finger and thumb close to the canvas, straightening it as necessary as you pull it through.

Ribbon is very strong, and it is not possible to stitch through it with a tapestry needle. Where the needle comes up in a hole already occupied by ribbon, take care to avoid trying to stitch through it, as this will spoil the appearance. Take the needle back and try again, coming up beside the existing stitch.

As ribbon may work a little loose during the embroidery, fasten off taking the needle behind several stitches on the back of the work, preferably tent stitch, if this has been used. Cut off the surplus, leaving a short end, so that this may be pulled up tight when the embroidery is finished.

Basket

This pretty embroidered basket will provide useful storage space for essential items in either the bedroom or bathroom. The pearl cotton with the wool background gives a pleasing contrast in texture.

Materials

Plastic canvas 7 bars per 1in
(2.5cm): one sheet
13½ x 10½in (34.5 x 26.5cm)
and one 4⅛in (10.5cm) circle
Paterna stranded wool, 8m
skeins: six 263 cream
Anchor No. 5 pearl cotton, 5gm
skeins: two each of 10 dark
peach, 08 light peach and 216
green, and one each of 942
honey and 295 yellow

Preparation

1 Cut the plastic canvas to
give one side 90 x 14 bars,
one backing strip 8 x 14, one
lining 89 x 13 bars, and one
handle 64 x 6 bars.

Working the embroidery

2 Work in small cross stitch
using 2 strands of wool or a
double thickness of pearl cotton.
For the handle, leaving the first
and last 4 bars uncovered, work
the embroidery from the chart.
Edge stitch each edge beside
the embroidery in cream.

3 For the side, tack (baste)
the handle to the exact
centre of one long edge of the
side section, underlapping it
by 4 bars. This will be the
wrong side now. The embroidery
will be worked through both
layers, joining the handle in
as you work. Tack (baste) the
backing strip to the back of
the right-hand short edge,
underlapping it by 4 bars.

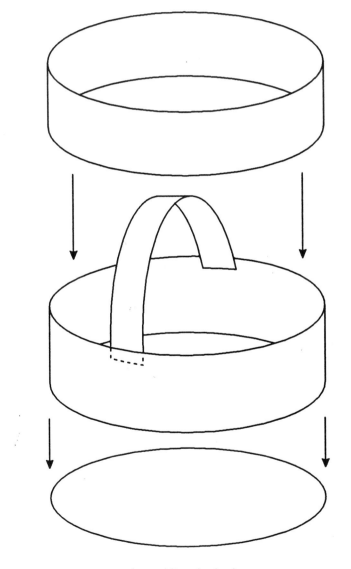

Assembling the basket

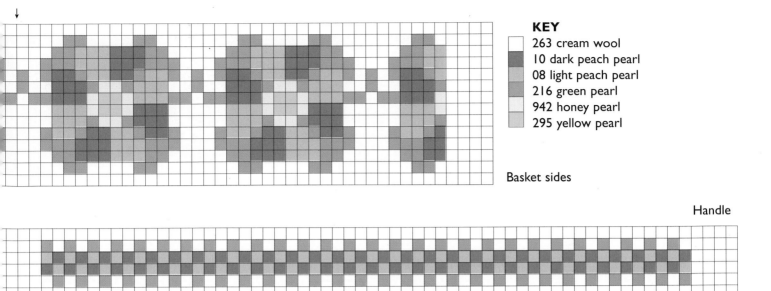

KEY

	263 cream wool
	10 dark peach pearl
	08 light peach pearl
	216 green pearl
	942 honey pearl
	295 yellow pearl

Basket sides

Handle

4 Leaving the first and 4 last bars uncovered, work the embroidery from the chart. With the right side of the embroidery outside, lap the left edge over the backing strip and tack (baste) in place. Tack the free end of the handle centrally over the join, underlapping it by 4 bars. Complete the embroidery through the 3 layers, so joining the side into a ring.

5 For the lining, leaving the first and last 4 bars uncovered, work lines of alternating satin stitch to cover the lining. As there are an odd number of bars, fill in with one line of tent stitch. With the right side inside, lap the left edge over the right and complete the embroidery through both layers, so making a ring. Overcast one edge.

6 For the base, you will need to work 2 stitches into one hole at intervals in order to keep the stitches looking the

same, as the number of holes in a plastic canvas circle decreases towards the centre. Leaving the outer bar uncovered, work rounds of satin and tent towards the centre as follows:

satin in cream over 2 bars
tent stitch in green
tent stitch in dark peach
tent stitch in light peach
satin stitch in cream over 3 bars
tent stitch in green
satin stitch in cream over 2 bars
tent stitch in light peach
tent stitch in green with a cross stitch over the centre.

Finishing

7 With the right side of the base uppermost, overcast the embroidered side in place, using the full 3 strands of wool. Slip the lining into the basket, covered edge to the base, and edge stitch round the top to join the 2 sections, overcasting through the handle as you do so.

Basket size

Baskets may be made in any size required up to 12in (30cm), which is the largest plastic canvas circle available at present. If the pre-formed sizes available are not the size you require, a larger circle may be used and cut down to size. This basket is based on a 4¼in (10.5cm) mesh circle and the side is lined with a second piece of canvas to give a strong and neat finish. The handle fits between the layers.

Picture frame

The frame is made from two pieces of canvas, the photograph fitting between. There is no need to embroider the back of this frame, so materials are given for working the embroidery on the front only.

Materials

Plastic canvas 7 bars per 1in
(2.5cm): one sheet
13½ x 10½in (34.5 x 26.5cm)
Offray ribbon 3mm wide: 5½yds
(5m) 815 cream
Anchor No. 5 pearl cotton, 5gm
skeins: two 214 green

Preparation

1 Cut 2 pieces of plastic canvas 44 x 36 bars. On one piece, mark the centre line of holes in both directions with a line of tacking (basting) stitches.

Working the embroidery

2 Work in the order given here, in tent and satin stitch, using either the ribbon or 3 thicknesses of pearl cotton. The central hole is cut after the embroidery is completed.

3 First work the rectangle of tent stitch in green pearl all the way round over the bar next to the edge. Work the ribbon embroidery in satin stitch, taking a length of 1⅜yds (1.25m), which will do one quarter. Next work the green triangles in pearl cotton in satin stitch. Inside this, work another line of tent stitch.

Finishing

4 Cut away the central uncovered area (see diagram), taking care to leave one bar beside the embroidery. Overcast in 3 strands of pearl

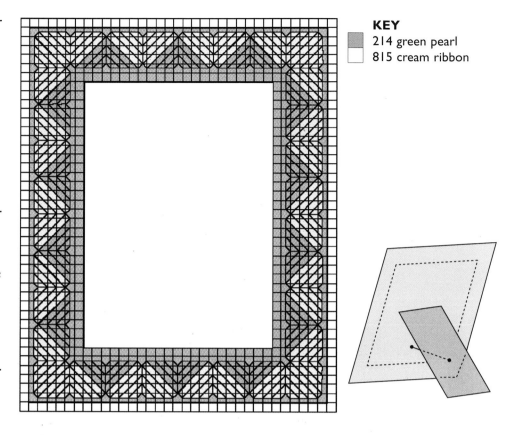

KEY
214 green pearl
815 cream ribbon

cotton. Work edge stitch along one short edge of the embroidered section and one short edge of the second piece.

5 Place the 2 pieces together, embroidered side outside, edges matched up, and work edge stitch round the top and sides to join them.

6 To make the stand, trim off the butts from the central piece. Place it on the back of the frame, one short edge centrally against the open edge, and stitch along the other short edge to make a stand.

7 Make a loop of doubled pearl cotton between the stand and the back of the frame, to prevent it opening out too far when in use, and test it for length

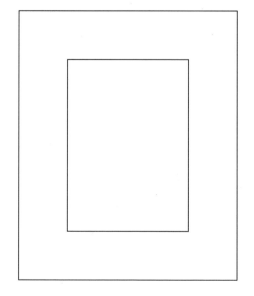

before tying the knots and trimming the surplus cotton.

8 Insert the photograph of your choice, then catch stitch invisibly along the lower edge to close the opening.

Manicure box

The box is made with a rising lining over which the lid fits. When the lid is removed the sides drop down to reveal the contents. The design is based on a motif found on an old sampler.

Materials

Plastic canvas 7 bars per 1in
(2.5cm): one sheet of ultra stiff
18 x 12in (46 x 30cm)
Paterna stranded wool, 8m
skeins: six each of 263 cream
and 481 terracotta, and two
603 green
Anchor No. 5 pearl cotton, 5gm
skeins: four 10 dark peach,
two 09 mauve, one each of 977
blue, 305 yellow, 108 light
mauve and 07 magenta
2mm card: one piece 12in
(30cm) square
1mm card: one piece 10 x 5in
(25 x 12.5cm)
Lining: cotton or polycotton
39 x 6½in (99 x 16.5cm)
Terylene wadding: 30 x 5in
(75 x 12.5cm)
1yd (90cm) elastic, ⅜in (1cm)
wide
Latex or clear adhesive

Making up the lid

Preparation

1 Cut the plastic canvas for
the outer box to give four
sides 28 x 35 bars, four lid sides
35 x 7 bars, and a base and lid
each 35 bars square. For the
inner box, cut one base 19 bars
square, four sides 19 x 13 bars,
and inner dividers one 18 x 12
bars, two 9 x 12 bars and one 12
bars square.

Working the embroidery

2 The borders are worked in
tent stitch and the main
area in small cross stitch. Work
with 2 strands of wool or a
double thickness of pearl cotton.
To keep the pattern correct
where the lid meets the box side,
2 stitches should be worked over
the edge in the appropriate

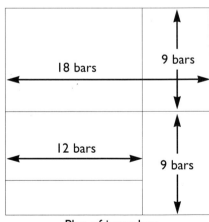

18 bars

9 bars

12 bars

9 bars

Plan of inner box

Cutting the lining

colour. On the charts these are shown like a normal stitch. This avoids fastening on for single stitches when finishing the edges later.

3 Embroider the sides, lid sides and top, following the charts on page 23. Embroider the outer base, if wished. Cover the sections for the inner box with tent stitch, leaving uncovered the bars on the base for attaching the dividers as shown on the diagram on page 21.

Finishing

4 For the lid, lay one lid side against the square lid, right sides outside, uncovered edges matched up, and edge stitch to join. Repeat with the other 3 sides. Edge stitch the corners to join, then edge stitch all round, taking the wool behind the coloured stitches which are already in place.

5 For the outer box, leaving the lower edges uncovered, work edge stitch round 3 sides of each of the 4 main side sections. Lay one side against the base, right sides outside, uncovered edges matched up, and edge stitch to join. Repeat with the other 3 sides.

6 For the inner box, overcast the dividers of the inner box to the inner base along the uncovered bars. To enable the sections to fit between the outer sides without bulging, they have been cut one bar narrower than the section to which they are being joined. Keep the joining

stitches at a moderately loose tension, so that when making up they adjust to allow the section to fit centrally.

7 Place the sides in position in turn and join them to the relevant dividers, making sure the stitches look like tent stitch on the right side, using a single strand of wool. Join the sides to the base by overcasting all round the lower edge. Join the corners. Overcast all round the top edge in cream, securing the top of the dividers as you do so.

8 For the lining, cut 4 pieces 4⅞ x 4½in (12.3 x 11.4cm) from the 2mm card. From the 1mm card, cut two 5in (12.5cm) squares. Cut the elastic into 4 equal pieces.

9 Using the card as a guide, cut the lining fabric as shown in the diagram on page 21. There should be approximately 1½in (4cm) between the sections, half that along the lower edge and 1½in (4cm) along the top. Using the card as guide, cut 4 pieces of wadding the size of the 2mm card.

10 Place one square piece of lining fabric, right side down, and place one of the 1mm squares of card centrally over it. Trim the corners, fold the turnings over the card and stick in place. Repeat with the second square. Spread adhesive round the edges on the wrong side of one piece, then place inside the lid and press in place until bonded. Spread adhesive on the other piece in the same way and

place it over the wrong side of the base, holding it firmly in place until bonded.

11 Lay a piece of fabric for the sides, right side down with the wadding over it, having ⅜in (2cm) for turning on 3 sides and 1½in (4cm) along one short edge. Place one of the pieces of card over the wadding. Trim the corners. Fold the turnings over the card and stick in position, taking particular care to make the larger turning look neat, as this will be visible above the embroidered side of the box. Repeat the same process for the other 3 sides.

12 Tie the elastic over one side, and adjust the length as necessary. Stitch it into a ring and place centrally over the side, with the join on the wrong side. Repeat for the other 3 sides.

13 Spread adhesive all round the edge of each side section, taking care not to get any on the right side. Place centrally on the back of each side piece of the outer box, with the lower edges level with the line of tent stitch. This should be about ⅛in (3mm) from the edge at the base and extend ⅜in (2cm) at the top. Before allowing it to bond, close the box to check that there is sufficient space for the sides to close properly. Weight each piece with a book, or something similar, to hold it firmly and ensure a good bond.

14 Stick the inner box centrally to the base to complete the box.

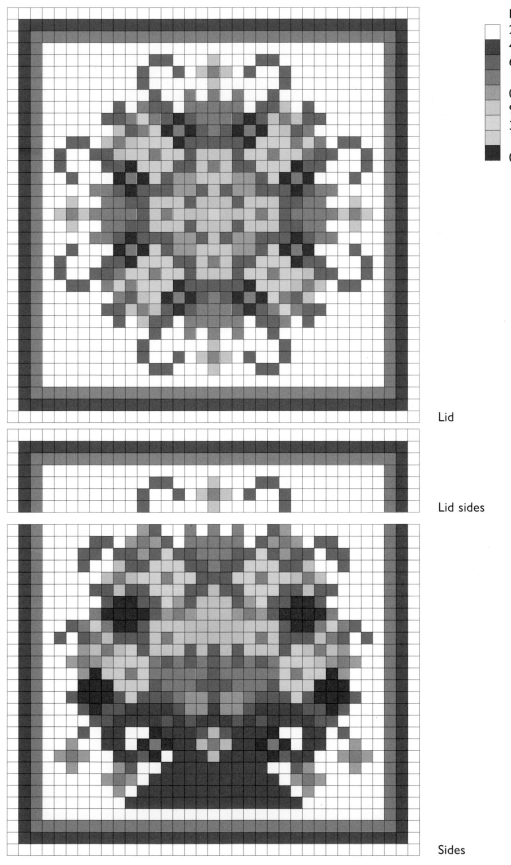

Lid

Lid sides

Sides

KEY

	263 cream wool
	481 terracotta wool
	603 green wool
	10 dark peach pearl
	09 mauve pearl
	977 blue pearl
	305 yellow pearl
	108 light mauve pearl
	07 magenta pearl

Living Room

Plant holder • Waste paper bin
Playing cards box • Spectacles case
Bookmarks

Plant holder

This fits a 5in (12.5cm) pot or a saucer holding a smaller pot. The base is a single circle of mesh which is not embroidered. The side is lined as for the bin on page 28 but without the facing.

Materials

Plastic canvas 7 bars per 1in
(2.5cm): one sheet
22½ x 13½in (57 x 34.5cm)
and one 6in (15cm) circle
Paterna stranded wool, 8m
skeins: six each of 510 dark
blue and 445 cream, two 511
medium blue and three 553
bright blue
Anchor No. 5 pearl cotton, 5gm
skeins: one 372 beige
Plastic-coated lining fabric:
18 x 4in (45 x 10cm)

Preparation

1 From the plastic canvas, cut
one side piece 124 x 27
bars. Using this a guide, cut the
lining fabric to the same size.

2 Then trim off a bare ⅛in
(3mm) from one long side.
When this is used to line the
main section there needs to be
room for the needle to pass
through when finishing the edge
and stitching the base on.

Working the embroidery

3 Leaving the first and last 4
bars uncovered, work the
embroidery in small cross stitch,
following the chart.

4 Overlap the uncovered
edges, matching up the
bars, and complete the
embroidery through both layers,
to join it into a ring.

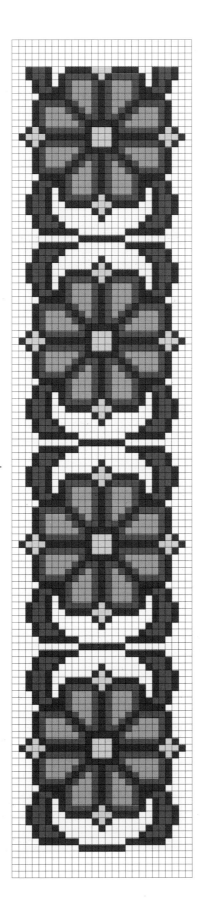

Finishing

5 Place the piece of lining
fabric inside the sleeve,
overlapping the edges. Slip
stitch round the upper and
lower edges, stretching the
fabric slightly as you stitch.
There is no need to stitch the
overlap in place. Use a little
adhesive, if wished.

6 Place the sleeve over the
circle and overcast to join
them. Edge stitch the upper
edge.

KEY
 372 beige pearl
510 dark blue wool
511 medium blue wool
553 bright blue wool
445 cream wool

Waste paper bin

The bin is made in three sections, an outer embroidered sleeve, an inner sleeve lined with plastic-coated fabric, and a facing attached to the outer sleeve and covering the top of the lining to give a neat finish.

Materials

Plastic canvas 7 bars per 1in (2.5cm): two sheets of ultra stiff canvas 22½ x 13½in (57 x 34cm), two plastic canvas circles 9½in (24cm) in diameter

Paterna stranded wool, 8m skeins: nine each of 445 cream and 510 dark blue, four 511 medium blue and three 553 bright blue

Anchor No. 5 pearl cotton, 5gm skeins: two each of 885 cream and 372 beige

PVC-coated cloth: 24 x 10in (60 x 25cm) blue or beige to tone with the main colours

Sewing thread to match the dark blue wool

Preparation

1 Cut one sheet of plastic canvas to give one main piece 151 x 63 bars, one facing 146 x 10 bars, one backing strip 63 x 8 bars and one 10 x 8 bars. From the second sheet, cut one lining 150 x 52 bars.

Working the embroidery

2 For the outer sleeve of the bin, tack (baste) the backing strip to the right-hand short edge of the main section. This will be the wrong side. Leaving the first and last 4 bars uncovered, work the embroidery in small cross stitch, following the chart on page 30.

3 Overlap the left edge over the backing strip, matching up the bars, and complete the embroidery through both layers, joining it into a sleeve.

4 For the facing, tack (baste) the backing strip to the right-hand edge of the facing section. This will be the wrong side. Leaving the first and last 4 bars uncovered, work lines of cross stitch in dark blue to cover, as shown on page 30. With the right side inside, overlap the left edge over the backing strip, matching up the bars, and complete the embroidery through both layers to join it into a ring. Overcast round one edge.

Finishing

5 Using the lining canvas as a guide, cut the PVC fabric, allowing ⅝in (1.5cm) extra for turnings at the side edges and 1in (2.5cm) at the top edge. No turning is necessary at the lower edge. Overlap by 4 bars and join the canvas into a ring, stitching securely to join.

6 Place the lining fabric inside the canvas lining, with the lower edge just above the outer bar. There needs to be room for the needle to pass through when stitching on the base. The vertical edges should overlap by about ⅝in (1.5cm). The lining will extend above the canvas at the top edge by about 1in (2.5cm). Slip stitch around the lower edge, taking the stitches over every other bar of the canvas, and stretching the fabric slightly as you stitch. Glue the overlap in place.

7 Trim the outer edge of the 2 circles, removing a frame 8 bars wide on one, and 7 bars wide on the other. (The frames are not needed for this project and may be stored for future use.) Trim the spikes off the circles.

8 Cut 2 circles of PVC lining fabric to fit the trimmed canvas circles. The edge should be between the 2 outer bars of the canvas circles, to allow the needle to pass through when stitching up. The neatest way to do this is to find a plate or something similar that is the correct size, draw round it and

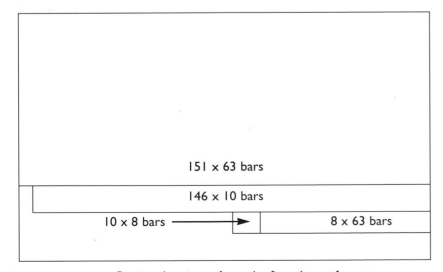

151 x 63 bars

146 x 10 bars

10 x 8 bars ———→   8 x 63 bars

Cutting the pieces from the first sheet of canvas

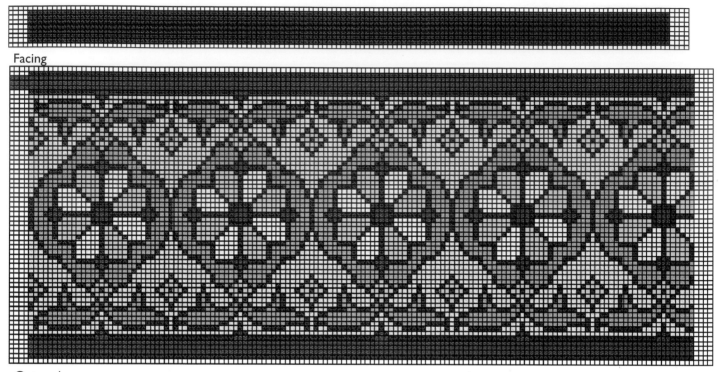

Facing

Outer sleeve

KEY

	445 cream wool
	510 dark blue wool
	511 medium blue wool
	553 bright blue wool
	885 cream pearl
	372 beige pearl

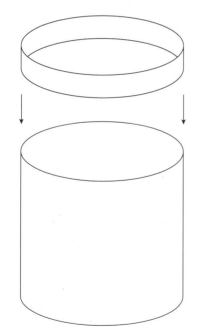

Slipping the facing into the outer sleeve

cut out. Alternatively, draw round the canvas circle, then cut out just inside the line. Slip stitch the PVC to the appropriate canvas circles.

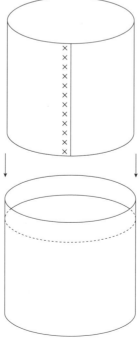

Lining the inner sleeve

9 Place the smaller of the circles, covered side up, with the prepared lined canvas sleeve over it. Overcast round the lower edge to join the two together. Place the larger circle, covered side down, with the embroidered sleeve over it. Overcast round the lower edge to join the two together.

10 Slip the facing into the top of the embroidered outer bin, matching up the uncovered edges, and edge stitch all round the top to join. Slip the prepared lining inside the bin and push the excess lining fabric up inside the facing.

Using the ultra stiff variety of plastic canvas for both the outer and inner sleeve makes further stiffening unnecessary, saving you the trouble of finding a suitable tin to cover.

Playing cards box

Just the right size to hold two packs of cards, score pads and pencils, this box has a lid which lifts off and acts as a tray. If you don't want to use it for cards, it can be used to hold other treasures.

Materials

Plastic canvas 10 bars per 1in
(2.5cm): two sheets
13½ x 10½in (34.5 x 26.5cm)
Paterna stranded wool, 8m
skeins: seven 510 dark blue,
five 511 medium blue and
three each of 553 bright blue
and 445 cream
Anchor No.5 pearl cotton, 5gm
skeins: one each of 885 cream
and 372 beige
2mm card: one piece 18 x 12in
(46 x 30cm)
1mm card: one piece 9 x 5in
(23 x 12cm)
Lining: cotton or polycotton
28 x 10½in (70 x 26.5cm)
Latex or clear adhesive

Preparation

1 Cut the plastic canvas to
give a lid, an underlid and a
base each 89 x 49 bars, two
sides 89 x 23 bars, two sides 49
x 23 bars, two lid lips 85 x 5
bars and two lid lips 45 x 5 bars.

Working the embroidery

2 Work in small cross stitch
throughout, using a single
strand of wool or pearl cotton.
Follow the charts for the upper
lid and sides. Embroider the
base with the initials and date
required, or in the lid pattern.

3 Work a rectangle of tent
stitch round the edge of the
underlid, next to the outer bar.
Cover the 4 lid lips with lines of
tent stitch in dark blue.

Finishing

4 Place one long side of the
box against the base, right
sides outside, edges matched up,
and edge stitch to join. Repeat
for the other 3 sides. Edge stitch
the corners to make into a box
shape. Edge stitch all round top.

5 Overcast the lid lips to the
underlid through the bar
next to the tent stitch. Overcast
all round the lip edge, joining the
corners as you do so.

Lining the box

6 Cut the 2mm card to give
two pieces 8¾ x 2⅛in
(22.2 x 5.4cm), two pieces
4½ x 2⅛in (11.5 x 5.4cm) and one
piece 8⅝ x 4½in (22 x 11.5cm).
Cut the 1mm card to give one
piece 8¼ x 4¼in (21 x 10.5cm).
Using the card as a guide, cut
fabric to cover each piece,
allowing ⅝in (1.5cm) extra all
round for turnings.

7 Place one piece of the
lining fabric right side down
with the appropriate piece of

45 x 5	45 x 5	
49 x 23	49 x 23	
89 x 49 bars	89 x 49 bars	85 x 5 / 85 x 5

89 x 49 bars	89 x 23	89 x 23

Cutting the canvas

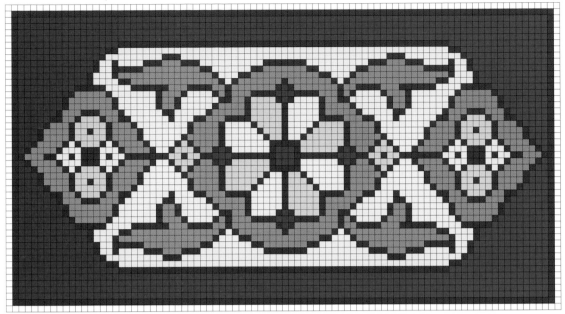

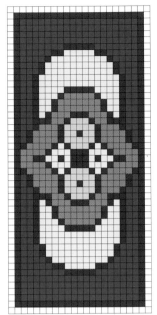

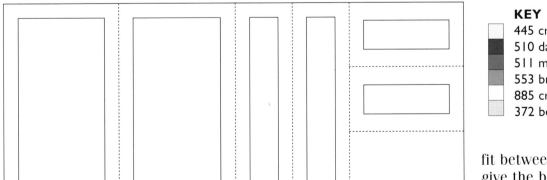

KEY

	445 cream wool
	510 dark blue wool
	511 medium blue wool
	553 bright blue wool
	885 cream pearl
	372 beige pearl

Cutting the lining

card placed centrally over it. Trim all the corners. Fold the lining turnings over the piece of card, short sides first, and stick in place. Repeat the same process for the other pieces of lining fabric and card.

8 Spread adhesive along the wrong side edges of the long side lining sections. Position them in the box, and use clothes pegs or something similar to hold them in place until bonded. Repeat for the short sides. These fit between the long sides and give the box rigidity. Slip the base into the box.

9 Slip stitch the thinner lined card to the back of the underlid. It fits snugly between the lid lips. Place the lid and the underlid together, right sides outside and edges matched up, and edge stitch all round to join together.

Spectacles case

Two sections of canvas are embroidered and then each piece is lined before stitching the two together to make an attractive spectacles case.

Materials

Plastic canvas with 10 bars per
1in (2.5cm): one sheet
13½ x 10½in (34.5 x 26.5cm)
Paterna stranded wool, 8m
skeins: two 444 beige, one
each of 510 dark blue, 502
medium blue, 553 bright blue,
and one 603 green
Lining: lightweight cotton or
polycotton 9in (23cm) square
Sewing thread to tone with the
dark blue wool

Preparation

1 From the plastic canvas, cut
two pieces 70 x 35 bars.

Working the embroidery

2 Work in small cross stitch,
using a single strand of
wool. Following the chart, work
the embroidery on both sections.

Finishing

3 Cut the lining fabric into 2
equal pieces. Fold and press
a turning of ⅝in (1.5cm) to the
wrong side on 2 adjacent edges
of one piece. Finger-press the
other 2 turnings, so that these
may be adjusted later, if
necessary. Trim the corners.
Place on the wrong side of one
embroidered section and tack
(baste) the 2 pressed edges in
place. The fold should lie just
inside the outer bar, allowing
room for the needle to pass
through when stitching up. Tack
(baste) the other 2 edges,

adjusting the turnings to give the
correct fit should this be
necessary, and trimming off any
excess turning.

4 Slip stitch the lining in
place, taking the stitches
over alternate bars of the plastic
canvas between the edge stitch
and the embroidery. These

stitches should merge with the
embroidery on the right side
and be almost invisible.

5 Edge stitch the upper 2
short edges. Lay the 2
sections together, right sides
outside, and edge stitch round
the 3 uncovered edges to join the
2 sections together.

KEY
444 beige wool
510 dark blue wool
502 med. blue wool
553 bright blue wool
603 green wool

Bookmarks

Bookmarks are the perfect small gift for anyone who likes books. They are especially suitable for children to make, being small and quickly made. They are also a good way of using up oddments of wool.

Materials

Plastic canvas 10 bars per 1in
    (2.5cm): one piece 68 x 14
    bars
Paterna stranded wool, 8m
    skeins: one each of 445 cream
    and 510 dark blue
Anchor No. 5 pearl cotton, 5gm
    skeins: one each of 19 red and
    492 honey

Preparation

1 Trim off any butts from the
    piece of plastic canvas.

Working the embroidery

2 Work in small cross stitch,
    using a single strand of
wool or pearl cotton. Following
the chart on the left, work the
dark blue pattern first to
establish the design.

Finishing

3 Work edge stitch in cream
    all the way round the edge.

Making a knotted fringe

4 To make a knotted fringe
    along one short edge, thread
a needle with a single strand of
cream wool, about 18in (46cm)
in length. Pull it through so that
the ends are together. Take the
needle down from the front
between the 2 left-hand bars of
the bookmark. Pull it through to
leave an end of about 2in (5cm).
Bring it up again one bar to the

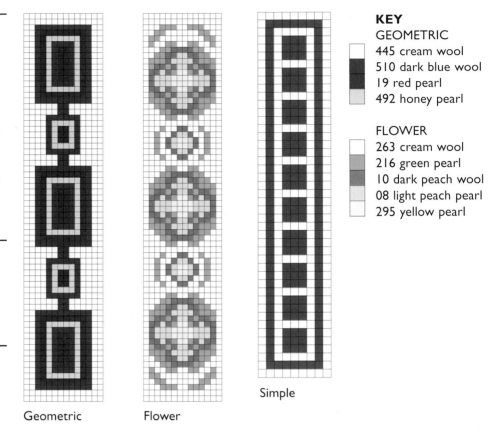

Geometric   Flower

Simple

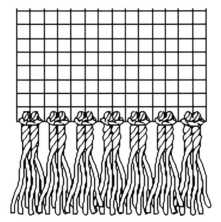

right, pulling it through so that
the ends and loop are equal in
length, and cut the wool. Slip the
ends through the loop and pull up
tightly, so that the knot lies
against the edge. Repeat to make
7 knots in all. Smooth the ends
and cut off the surplus to give a
neat finish.

Flower bookmark

This is made from the same size
canvas as the geometric design.
You will need Paterna stranded
wool, 8m skein: one 263 cream,
and Anchor No. 5 pearl cotton,
5gm skeins: one 10 dark peach,
one 08 light peach, one 295
yellow and one 216 green.

Simple bookmark

This is a really simple design,
ideal for children to enjoy
making. You will need 7 count
canvas measuring 45 x 9 bars
and about 10yds (10m) knitting
wool in two colours.

Kitchen and Dining Room

Kitchen notepad holder
Egg cosies and small basket
Tablemat • Napkin rings • Coasters

Kitchen notepad holder

A kitchen notepad holder is both useful and decorative. This one is made in two sections, the embroidered front with a slit to take the notepad, and a back section which is not embroidered.

Materials

Plastic canvas 7 bars per 1in
(2.5cm): one sheet 12 x 18in
(30 x 46cm)
Paterna stranded wool, 8m
skeins: five 553 blue, one each
of 611 dark green and 613
grass green
Anchor No. 5 pearl cotton, 5gm
skeins: one each of 74 light
pink, 75 dark pink and 942
yellow
2 small curtain rings or sticky-
back magnets
5 x 8in (13 x 20cm) notepad

Preparation

1 Cut the plastic canvas to
give two pieces 73 x 53
bars. At one end (which will be
the top), cut an aperture one bar
wide, leaving 10 bars above the
opening and 10 bars on each side
(see chart). Trim off the spikes.

Working the embroidery

2 Following the chart, work
the embroidery pattern in
small cross stitch, filling in the
central area with alternating
satin stitch over 2 bars, with a
single row of tent stitch over the
centre bar.

Finishing

3 Overcast all round the
opening in blue wool. Attach
the curtain rings or magnets to
the second piece of mesh, just
below the top edge and 1–2in
(2.5–5cm) in from the side edges.

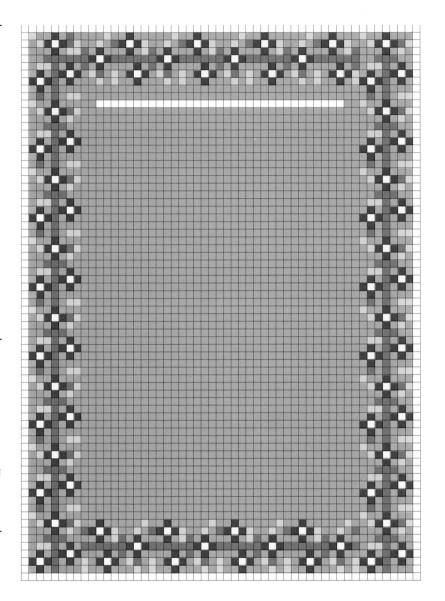

4 Place the embroidered
section over the second
piece, right sides outside, and
edge stitch all round to join
together. Put the pad in place
and hang it in your chosen spot.

How to hang the notepad holder

The holder may be fixed to the
fridge door with magnets, or
hung on the wall by two curtain
rings, sewn on before making up
the holder.

KEY
553 blue wool
611 dark green wool
613 grass green wool
74 light pink pearl
75 dark pink pearl
942 yellow pearl

Egg cosies and small basket

These fun items will brighten up an Easter breakfast table. The little basket is quick to make and, filled with Easter eggs, would delight any small girl. The materials listed will make four egg cosies.

Materials

For egg cosies
Plastic canvas 7 bars per 1in
(2.5cm): one sheet 18 x 12in
(46 x 30cm)
Paterna stranded wool, 8m
skeins: five green 602 and one
716 cream
Anchor No. 5 pearl cotton, 5gm
skeins: two 306 dark yellow,
one each of 386 cream, 214
green, and 295 light yellow

For the basket
Plastic canvas with 7 bars per
1in (2.5cm): half a sheet
13½ x 10½in (34.5 x 26.5cm)
and one 3in (7.5cm) circle
Paterna stranded wool, 8m
skeins: one each of 263 cream
and 603 green
Anchor No. 5 pearl cotton, 5gm
skeins: one each of 295 light
yellow and 306 dark yellow

MAKING THE EGG COSIES

Preparation

1 Cut the sheet of plastic
canvas into 16 pieces each
24 x 15 bars.

Working the embroidery

2 Work the border at top and
base in long cross stitch,
the central pattern in small cross
stitch. Use 2 strands of wool or a
double thickness of pearl cotton.
Start with the lines of green long
cross stitch (see chart on page
44). Bring the needle up on the
left edge, 7 bars up from the
base and 2 bars to the right for
the first stitch. Work diagonally
down to the centre of the lower
edge, and then up to the right.
Do the same for the second line
of green. This will establish the
pattern.

3 Inside this, work a line in
cream pearl long cross
stitch. Fill in the 2 lower corner
triangles with green pearl long
cross stitch. Work the centre
pattern from the chart, in small
cross stitch.

Finishing

4 Trim off the surplus canvas
at the upper 2 corners (see
chart), taking care to leave one
bar beside the embroidery.
Overcast these trimmed corners,
using 2 strands of green wool.
This will ensure a good cover
when the edges are joined later.

5 Place 2 embroidered pieces
together, right sides outside,
and edge stitch one long edge to
join. Join other pieces in the
same way. Overcast the trimmed
overcast edges to join them. Edge
stitch round the lower edge in
green wool. Repeat to make 4
cosies.

MAKING THE SMALL BASKET

Preparation

6 From the half sheet of
canvas, cut one piece for
the side 64 x 10 bars and one
for the handle 40 x 5 bars. Tack
(baste) the handle to the centre
of the side piece of canvas,
underlapping it by 4 bars. This
will now be the wrong side. When
the embroidery is worked, the
stitches pass through both
layers, joining the handle to the
side.

Working the embroidery

7 Work the handle in long
cross stitch and the basket
side in small cross stitch, using 2
strands of wool or a double
thickness of pearl cotton. For the
handle, leaving 4 bars at the free
edge uncovered, work a line of
alternating long and short cross
stitch across the handle in green
wool. Repeat to fill in the spaces.
Edge stitch each edge beside the
embroidery in green pearl.

8 For the side, leaving the
first and last 4 bars
uncovered, work the pattern
following the chart on page 44.
Fill in the background with cream
cross stitch. With the right side
outside, lap the left edge over the
right, and tack (baste) in place.
Next, tack (baste) the handle in
place over the underlap.
Complete the embroidery through
all the layers.

9 For the base, work rounds
of satin stitch over 2 bars
in cream wool, starting over
the bars next to the edge and
finishing with a cross stitch over
the centre bars. You will need to
work 2 stitches into one hole at
intervals in order to keep the
stitches looking the same, as the
number of holes in a plastic
canvas circle decreases towards
the centre.

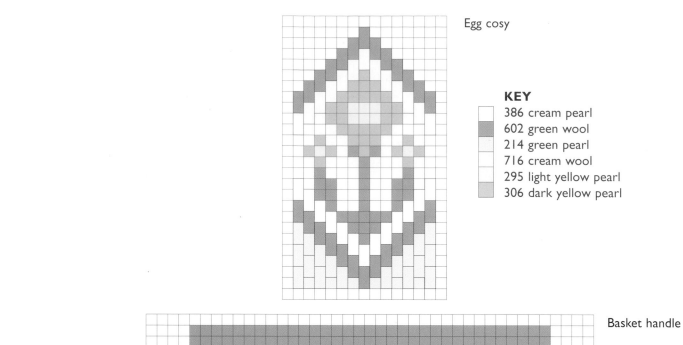

Egg cosy

KEY

	386 cream pearl
	602 green wool
	214 green pearl
	716 cream wool
	295 light yellow pearl
	306 dark yellow pearl

Basket handle

Basket sides

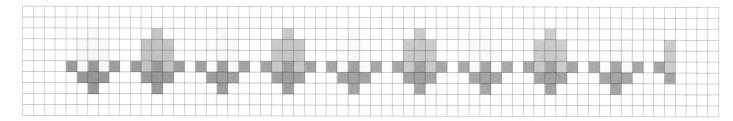

Finishing

10 Place the base, right side up with the side over it, and overcast all round to join the two together. Edge stitch all round the top.

Small basket

After the Easter festivities are over, the small basket can be used as an attractive cruet holder on your breakfast table.

Tablemat

The main design on this tablemat is worked in long cross stitch, with the cream background in small cross stitch. The mat does not have to be lined, but instructions are given for doing this, if so wished.

Materials

Plastic canvas 7 bars per 1in
(2.5cm): one sheet
13½ x 10½ in (34.5 x 26.5cm)
Paterna stranded wool, 8m
skeins: four 716 cream and
three 602 green
Anchor No. 5 pearl cotton, 5gm
skeins: four each of 214 green
and 386 cream, two of 295
light yellow and one of 306
dark yellow
Lining (optional): cotton or
polycotton 15 x 12in
(40 x 30cm)
Sewing thread to tone with the
light green pearl

Preparation

1 Cut one bar off the long
edge of the canvas to give a
piece 70 bars wide. Run a line of
tacking (basting) stitches through
the holes on each side of the
centre bar in the short direction,
and on each side of the 2 central
bars in the long direction.

Working the embroidery

2 The diamond pattern and
the border are worked in
long cross stitch, the pattern
inside the diamond shapes in
small cross stitch. Work with 2
strands of wool or a double
thickness of pearl cotton.

3 For the dark green lines,
start at the centre of the
canvas and work a long cross
stitch over the centre bars as
marked on the chart. Continue
stitching in a diagonal line to the

top right edge. Change direction
and then work 11 more stitches
to the right edge (A - B on the
chart). Repeat the process in the
other 3 directions.

4 Next, work long cross stitch
from the top right edge to
the lower edge (B - C), continue
up to the left edge (C - D), up to
the top edge (D - E) and down to
the right edge again at * marked
on the chart.

5 Repeat step 4 in reverse.
Starting at the top left edge,
work down to the lower edge,
continue up to the right edge, up
to the top edge, and down to the
left edge again to complete the
grid.

6 For the border, work a line
of long cross stitch in light
yellow pearl cotton next to the
triangles round the outer edge
of the embroidery. Fill in the
triangles with long cross stitch
in green pearl cotton.

7 For the central area, work
a line of long cross stitch
in cream pearl cotton inside the
diamond shapes. Work the large
flower pattern in the 10 outer
diamonds. Work the small flower
shape at the centre of the 8
central diamonds. Fill in the
background of the outer and
central diamonds with small
cross stitch in cream wool.

Finishing

8 Work edge stitch in green
pearl cotton all round the
outer edge.

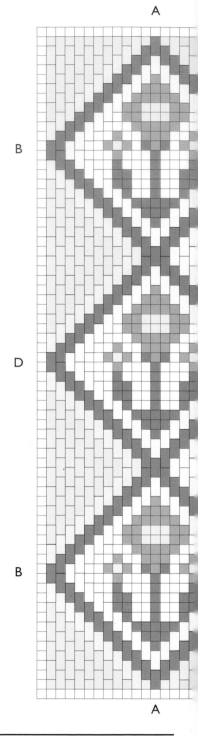

Lining (optional)

9 Fold and press a turning of
⅝in (1.5cm) to the wrong
side on one long and one short
edge of the lining fabric. Then
finger-press the other 2 turnings

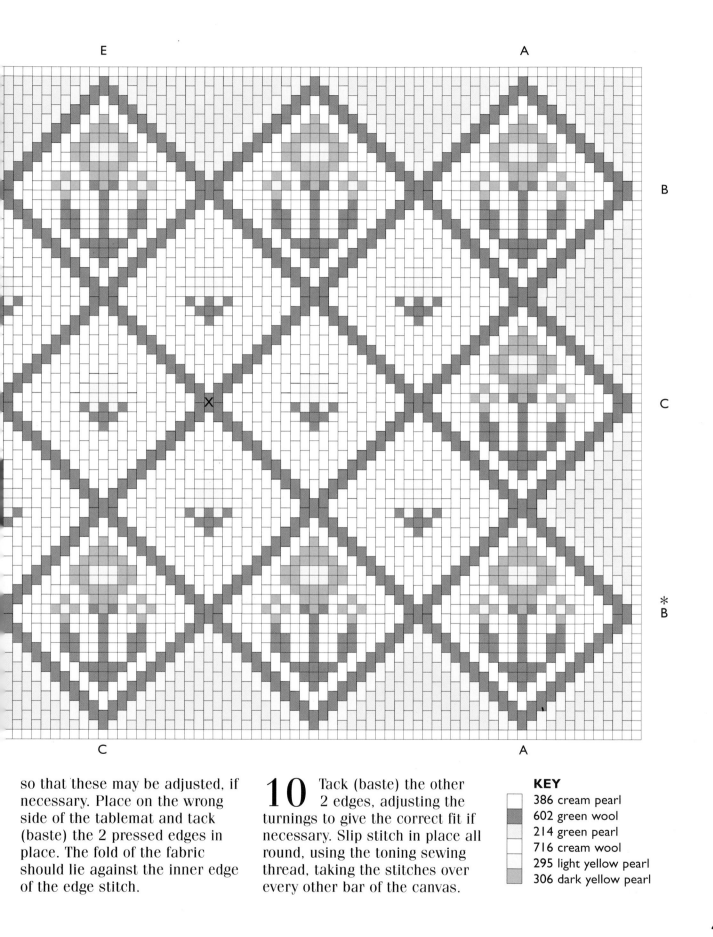

so that these may be adjusted, if necessary. Place on the wrong side of the tablemat and tack (baste) the 2 pressed edges in place. The fold of the fabric should lie against the inner edge of the edge stitch.

10 Tack (baste) the other 2 edges, adjusting the turnings to give the correct fit if necessary. Slip stitch in place all round, using the toning sewing thread, taking the stitches over every other bar of the canvas.

KEY
	386 cream pearl
	602 green wool
	214 green pearl
	716 cream wool
	295 light yellow pearl
	306 dark yellow pearl

47

Napkin rings

Four different colour designs are given here; if preferred you could make a matching set of napkin rings. The materials listed are enough to make four rings.

Materials

Plastic canvas 7 bars per 1in
(2.5cm): half a sheet
13½ x 10½in (34.5 x 26.5cm)
Paterna stranded wool, 8m
skeins: two 602 green and one
716 cream
Anchor No. 5 pearl cotton, 5gm
skeins: one each of 386 cream,
295 light yellow, 306 dark
yellow and 214 green

Preparation

1 Cut the plastic canvas
to give 4 pieces each
40 x 10 bars.

Working the embroidery

2 Work in long cross stitch
throughout, using 2 strands
of wool or a double thickness of
pearl cotton.

3 To avoid unnecessary
fastening off and on as you
work each colour, leave the
unused thread at the right-hand
edge, to be used when the canvas
is overlapped and the embroidery
is completed. Take care not to
stitch in these loose ends on the
back of the plastic canvas when
continuing to embroider the
design.

4 For each version of the
napkin ring design, be sure
to leave the first and last 4 bars
uncovered, then work the zig-zag
line and fill in, using the colours
specified on the right for each
version, following the appropriate
embroidery chart above.

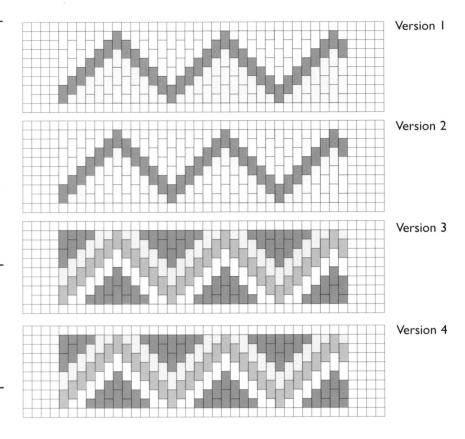

Version 1

Version 2

Version 3

Version 4

To finish

5 Overlap the 2 short edges of
the embroidery, matching up
the bars, and complete through
both layers, to join it into a ring.
Edge stitch round each edge in
green wool.

KEY

602 green wool,
386 cream pearl
716 cream wool
295 light yellow pearl
306 dark yellow pearl
214 green pearl

VERSION 1
Work the zig-zag line in green
wool. Fill in the triangles with
cream pearl cotton on one side
and yellow pearl on the other.
Finish as above.

VERSION 2
Work the zig-zag line in green
wool. Work a line on each side of
this, one in cream pearl cotton
and the other in light yellow
pearl. Fill in the triangles in
cream wool. Finish as above.

VERSION 3
Work the zig-zag line in light
yellow pearl cotton. Fill in the
triangles with cream pearl on one
side and green pearl on the
other. Finish as above.

VERSION 4
Work the zig-zag line in dark
yellow pearl cotton. Work a line
on each side of this, one in cream
pearl and the other in green
pearl. Fill in the triangles with
green wool. Finish as above.

Coasters

**The materials given are sufficient for four coasters.
It is not essential to line them, but instructions are given
so that you can line them, if wished.**

Materials

Plastic canvas 7 bars per 1in
  (2.5cm): one sheet
  13½ x 10½in (34.5 x 26.5cm)
Paterna stranded wool, 8m
  skeins: one each of 716 cream
  and 602 green
Anchor No. 5 pearl cotton, 5gm
  skeins: three 214 green, one
  each of 386 cream, 306 dark
  yellow and 295 light yellow
Lining (optional): lightweight
  cotton or polycotton 20 x 5in
  (50 x 12.5cm)
Sewing thread to tone with the
  green pearl cotton

Preparation

1 Cut the plastic canvas into 4
  pieces each 26 x 25 bars.
Tie a knot on the edge to mark
the centre bar of one short edge.
This will be the top of the
pattern.

Working the embroidery

2 Work the border in long
  cross stitch, and the central
pattern in small cross stitch. Use
2 strands of wool or a double
thickness of pearl cotton.
Starting at the knot at the top,
and following the chart, work a
diagonal line of long cross stitch
in green wool down to the centre
of the right-hand edge. Continue
down to the lower edge, up to the
left and complete the diamond
shape. Remove the marking knot.

3 Outside the green line, work
  lines of long cross stitch in
light yellow pearl. Fill in the

triangles at the corners with long
cross stitch in green pearl cotton.

4 Inside the diamond shape,
  work a line of long cross
stitch in cream pearl. Following
the chart, work the flower shape
at the centre in small cross
stitch. Fill in the background with
small cross stitch in cream wool.
Edge stitch all round in green
pearl.

Lining (optional)

5 Cut the lining fabric into 4
  equal pieces. Fold and press
a ⅝in (1.5cm) turning to the
wrong side on 2 adjacent edges
of one piece. Finger-press the
other 2 turnings, so that these
may be adjusted later, if
necessary. Trim the corners.

KEY

☐	386 cream pearl
▨	602 green wool
☐	214 green pearl
☐	716 cream wool
☐	295 light yellow pearl
▨	306 dark yellow pearl

Place on the wrong side of each
coaster and tack (baste) the 2
pressed edges in place. The fold
should lie against the inner edge
of the edge stitch. Tack (baste)
the other 2 edges, adjusting the
turnings to give the correct fit if
necessary, and trimming off any
excess turning.

6 Slip stitch in place, taking
  the stitches over alternate
bars of the canvas between the
edge stitch and the embroidery.
These stitches should merge with
the embroidery on the right side,
and be almost invisible.

Gift Ideas

Baby's carry bag • Sampler
Festive table runner
Tree decorations • Advent calendar

Baby's carry bag

This delightful bag has been designed to hold all the
essentials required by a mother on a day out with her baby.
Stiff mesh is recommended for the main sections, but soft
or standard mesh for the handle.

Materials

Ultra stiff plastic canvas with 7 bars per 1in (2.5cm): four sheets 18 x 12in (46 x 30cm)

Soft plastic canvas: one piece about 10in (25cm) long x 10 bars wide

Anchor tapisserie, 10m skeins: sixteen 8964 light jade, five 8938 dark jade, twelve 8006 cream, ten 8396 pale pink, nine each of 8626 blue and 8038 maize, two 9448 nutmeg, and one each of 8630 dark blue, 8436 dark pink and 8438 bright pink and a small amount of 9800 black

Velcro: the stitch-in hook-and-loop variety, about 1½in (4cm), 1in (2.5cm) wide

Latex or clear adhesive

Preparation

1 From the stiff plastic canvas, cut two pieces each 81 x 60 bars for the outer bag, four sides 81 x 10 bars and four sides 60 x 10 bars. For the inner lining, cut two main pieces 79 x 58 bars, two 79 x 16 and two 58 x 16. From the soft mesh, cut two handles 60 x 10 bars, three fastening strips 15 x 4 bars and four guides 11 x 4 bars.

Working the embroidery

2 For the outer bag, work the 2 main sections, 4 short sides, 4 long sides, 3 fastenings and the 4 guides in tent and satin stitch, following the charts on pages 56 and 57. Note that on each of 2 long bag sides 3 small sections are left uncovered for attaching the fastenings. Embroider the bears panel for each main section in cross stitch, following the chart on page 57.

3 Following the chart, embroider the 2 handles in tent and satin stitch. Cut away the surplus canvas, taking care to leave one bar beside the embroidery.

4 For the inner bag, cover the 6 sections with rows of random satin stitch in the 5 main colours, as shown on page 58, excluding the dark jade. Use each in turn, taking about 3 pulls from the skein. Keep an eye on the way the colours come together, fastening off and taking the next colour if this will improve the way they follow on.

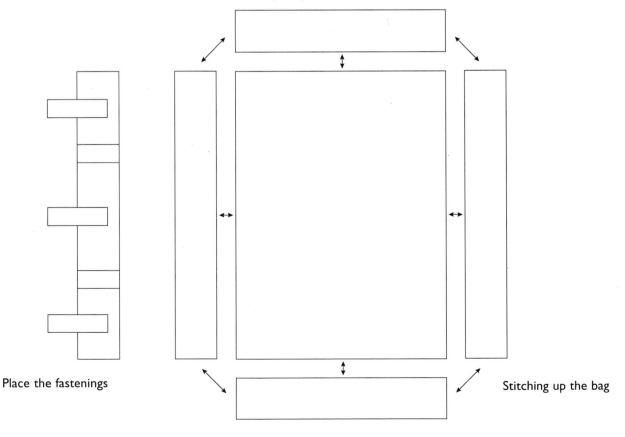

Place the fastenings

Stitching up the bag

Finishing

5 Using doubled light jade wool, sew up the bag.

6 To attach the handles and fastenings, tack (baste) the handle guides to the appropriate long sides, placing them 3in (7.5cm) in from each short edge, taking care that the guides are exactly square.

7 Cut 3 strips of velcro ⅜in (1cm) wide. Each strip should cover half a fastening section. Slip stitch the 3 hook sides in place on one end of each fastening, using matching sewing thread. Tack (baste) the 3 fastenings in position.

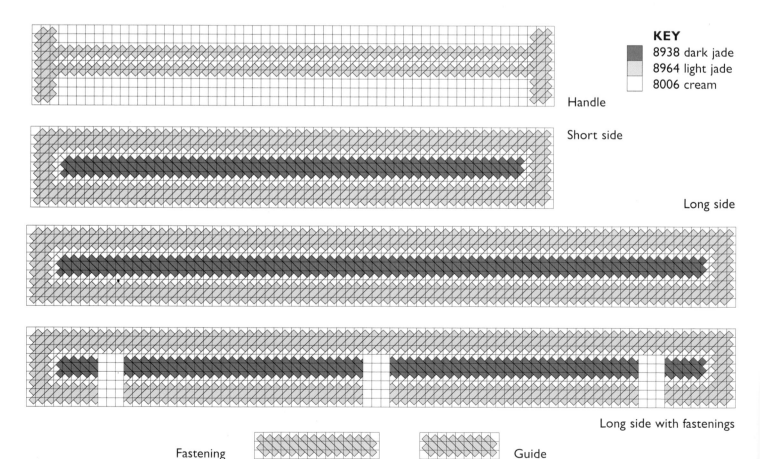

KEY

8938	dark jade
8964	light jade
8006	cream

Handle

Short side

Long side

Long side with fastenings

Fastening

Guide

KEY

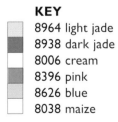

8964 light jade
8938 dark jade
8006 cream
8396 pink
8626 blue
8038 maize

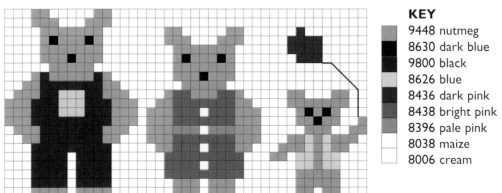

KEY

9448 nutmeg
8630 dark blue
9800 black
8626 blue
8436 dark pink
8438 bright pink
8396 pale pink
8038 maize
8006 cream

8 Overcast round the free edges, continuing the stitching round the edge, joining them to the box side. Slip stitch the 3 loop sections in place on the other relevant long side of the bag.

9 Next, stitch up the box. When stitching up the outer bag sections, make sure the heads of the teddy bears are towards the edge with the handles. Place the long side with the fastenings against the edge of the teddy bear section and overcast to join, going through the handle guide as you do so.

10 Without fastening off, continue joining the other 3 sides to the main section. Join the 4 corners to form a box shape. Repeat for the other main section.

11 Remove the tacking (basting) from the free edge of the handle guides, slip the handle in place and tack (baste) again. Overcast round 3 edges of the box, omitting the long edge opposite the handle, and joining the guides in as you go.

12 Using a single strand of wool, work an extra tent stitch over the existing one at each end of the handle guides. This will prevent the handles slipping through when the bag is in use. Repeat for the other section.

13 Place the 2 embroidered box shapes together, with the uncovered edges

matched up, and then overcast to join them, forming a hinge.

The lining

14 Overcast the 4 sides to one of the main lining pieces and join the corners to make a box shape. Overcast all round the upper edge. Spread adhesive evenly inside the edge of the side of the bag without the fastenings and place the prepared lining box in position. Hold the sections together until they are bonded.

15 Overcast all round the second flat lining piece and stick this to the back of the lid, holding it in place until it is securely bonded.

Velcro
You can use just the hook velcro and attach it to the embroidery, if preferred, but this is not quite so secure, and the hook-and-loop variety is recommended.

Sampler

Samplers make lovely gifts for a new baby, or interesting records of the life of an older child. They can incorporate a picture of the child's home, a family pet or favourite toy.

Materials

Plastic canvas 10 bars per 1in (2.5cm): one sheet approximately 13½ x 10½in (34.5 x 26.5cm). The Uniek variety measures 111 x 141 bars. If using Darice canvas, the border left for framing would be 2 bars narrower all round

Anchor stranded cotton, 8m skeins: two 216 dark green, two 203 light green, one each of 265 grass green, 75 pink, 168 blue, 167 light blue, 403 black, 400 dark grey, 850 medium grey, 398 light grey, 161 grey/blue, 369 terracotta, 891 medium yellow, 293 light yellow, 02 white, 375 brown, and 307 ginger

Small amounts of: 74 light pink (tree blossom), 46 red, 243 green, and 133 royal blue

Paterna stranded wool, 8m skeins: seven 263 cream

Preparation

1 To make identification easier, group the similar colours together. Mark the centre of the canvas in both directions with lines of tacking (basting) stitches on each side of the centre bars.

Working the embroidery

2 The design is worked in cross stitch using the full 6 strands of cotton, the background in tent stitch with 2 strands of cream wool. It is usual to start at the centre and work outwards, in order to minimise the possibility of mistakes in counting. With this design, work the horizontal section at the centre first.

3 Work the dark grey line over the centre bar and the line of flowers above it. Then work part of the vertical row of green cross stitch at each side. Work the rectangular border of flowers, working out from the centre of each long side.

4 Work the line of alternating dark and light green round the outer edge, again starting at the centre of the long sides. This should leave 5 or 3 bars uncovered all round, depending on the canvas used. Inside the flower border complete the rectangle of cross stitch in dark green. Fill in the background of the border in cream wool tent stitch.

5 The house and the teddy should be worked next, placing them exactly on the centre vertical line. The doors and windows on the house are worked in satin stitch.

6 Complete the remaining pattern, including the name and date, if known (see chart on page 62). Fill in the background in cream wool tent stitch.

7 The sampler can be framed as required. If you do not wish to have it framed, trim off the uncovered bars from the edges, taking care to leave one beside the embroidery. Trim off any butts and overcast all round in cream wool.

Sampler for a new baby

If the sampler is being prepared prior to the baby's birth, all the embroidery can be completed, leaving the name and date section to be filled in later. In this case, work the border flowers in alternating pink and blue, making it suitable for a girl or a boy.

KEY

- 263 cream wool
- 216 dark green cotton
- 203 light green cotton
- 265 grass green cotton
- 75 pink cotton
- 168 blue cotton
- 167 light blue cotton
- 403 black cotton
- 400 dark grey cotton
- 850 medium grey cotton
- 161 grey/blue cotton
- 375 brown cotton
- 891 medium yellow cotton
- 293 light yellow cotton
- 02 white cotton
- 398 light grey cotton
- 369 terracotta cotton
- 74 light pink cotton
- 46 red cotton
- 243 bright green cotton
- 133 royal blue cotton
- 307 ginger cotton

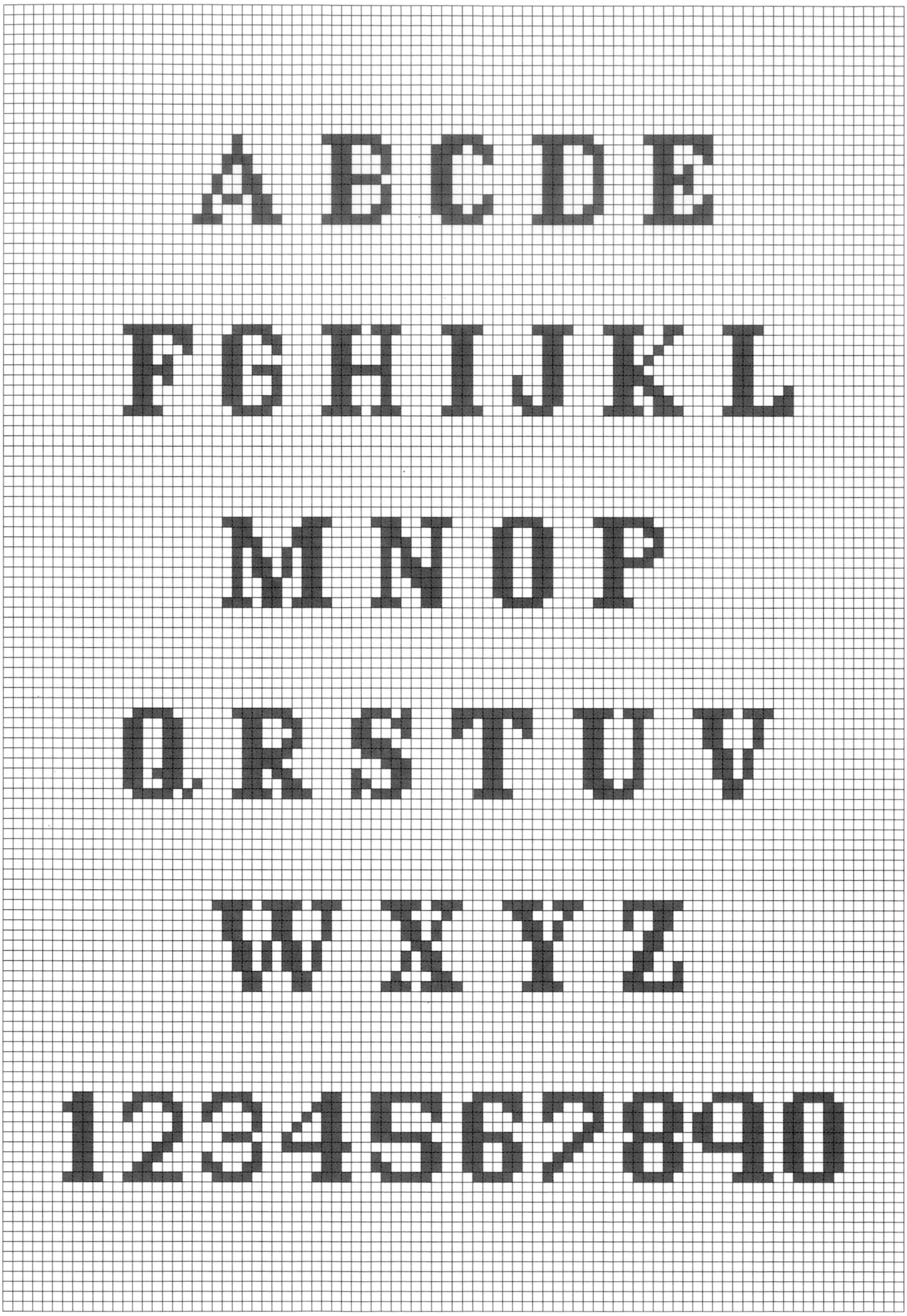

ABCDE
FGHIJKL
MNOP
QRSTUV
WXYZ
1234567890

Festive table runner

What better way to decorate the Christmas supper table than with this dramatic table centre? For the main meal it could be used on the sideboard, as hot dishes should not be put down on it unprotected.

Joining the canvas

The runner is made from two lengths of plastic canvas which are joined together by placing a backing strip behind the join, and embroidering through both layers. In this example the join is between the sixth and seventh patterns, the three lines of tent stitch giving maximum neatness to the join. For this reason the large sheets of plastic canvas are used. The smaller 18 x 12in (46 x 30cm) sheets could be used, with the join in a different place.

The pattern

There is a pretty 16th century carpet in Hatfield House in Hertfordshire, England, with a floral spray motif. The workers started at each end and when the middle was reached it was found that a mistake had been made in counting, and the central line of sprays had to be made smaller, rather marring the appearance of the carpet.

In order to avoid the possibility of a mistake in counting, the measurements given here allow several bars spare on the right section, which may be cut off, as directed, when the pieces are joined.

This runner is long, and when joined is quite heavy to handle. For this reason it is recommended that for comfort and convenience each piece should be worked separately, starting at opposite ends, and should be joined when the work is almost completed.

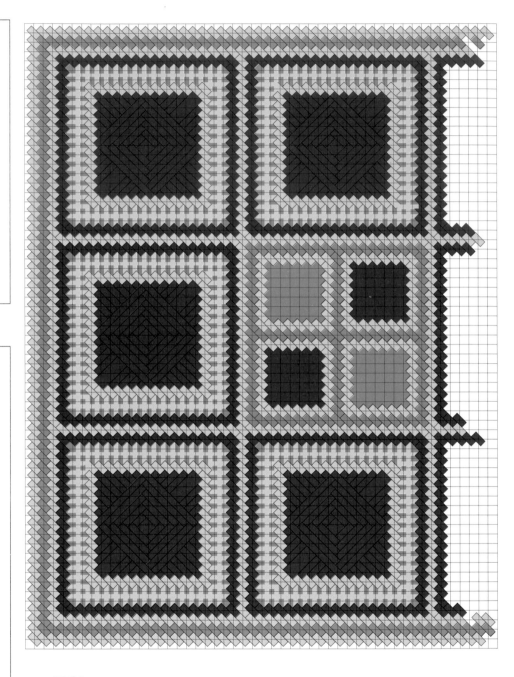

KEY

 Twilleys gold
46 red pearl
228 green pearl

Materials

Plastic canvas 7 bars per 1in
(2.5cm): two sheets
22½ x 13½in (57 x 34.5cm)
Anchor No. 5 pearl cotton, 5gm
skeins: six 46 red and five 228
green
Twilleys goldfingering: 25gm
balls: two 02 gold
Offray ribbon, 3mm wide: 42 yds
(38m) 250 red

Preparation

1 Cut the canvas to give one
piece 123 x 67 bars, one
piece 108 x 67 bars (a total of
227 bars is actually needed), and
one piece 8 x 67 bars for backing
the join. Tack (baste) the backing
strip to the right edge of the
longer section, underlapping it by
4 bars (the 2 pieces are not
joined together at this stage).

WORKING THE EMBROIDERY

The left-hand section

2 For the tent stitch border,
leave 4 bars of the backing
strip uncovered, and, starting at
the top right, work a line of tent
stitch in gold over the bar next
to the edge, across to the left
corner, down the left edge and
across the lower edge. Inside
this, work tent stitch in green.
Inside this, work gold tent stitch.

3 Starting from one short
side, work 5 vertical lines
in gold tent stitch, 19 bars apart
and starting 19 bars in from the
gold tent stitch border, following
the chart. Work 2 similar rows
in the long direction to within 4
bars of the right edge, leaving
the backing strip uncovered.
There will be 5 squares in the
long direction.

4 For the Norwich stitch
border, leave the 4 bars
of the backing strip, uncovered,
so that the sixth square will be
incomplete at this stage, then
continue as follows: inside each
outer square, work a square of
tent stitch in red. Next, work a
square of double cross stitch, in
green and gold, then a square
of tent stitch in gold. Fill in with
Norwich stitch in red ribbon.
There will be 6 Norwich stitches
in the long direction of this
section, and three in the short.

5 For the central area of the
table runner, inside each
square, work a square of tent
stitch in green, followed by a line
of tent stitch across the centre
bars in both directions, dividing
the area into 4 equal squares.
Work a square in gold inside
each. Fill in with 9 double cross
stitches, alternating red and
green pearl in the 4 squares.

The right-hand section

6 Embroider the right-hand
section in the same way as
the left-hand section, this time
leaving the left 8 bars uncovered.
Work the tent stitch as for the
left-hand section, this time
continuing down the right-hand
edge. Continue as before. There
will be 5 Norwich stitches in the
long direction of this section.

Finishing

7 The pieces can now be
joined, and the embroidery
completed through both layers.
There should be 9 bars between
the Norwich stitches where the
mesh is being joined. The canvas
will need to be overlapped by 4
bars, so lap the left edge of the
right section over the backing
strip to check on this. It should
be necessary to trim off the 4
surplus bars. Do this, or adjust
to give the correct pattern.

8 Complete the embroidery
through both layers. Work
edge stitch in red pearl all round.
If wished, line the back as for the
Tablemat (see page 46).

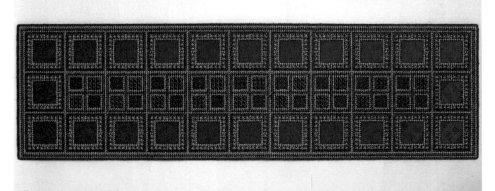

Tree decorations

These pretty tree decorations are made from a mixture of lustrous ribbon and pearl cotton, in different textured stitches. Two identical pieces are embroidered and then stitched together.

Materials

(enough for 14 decorations)
Plastic canvas 7 bars per 1in (2.5cm): one sheet 13½ x 10½in (34.5 x 26.5cm)
Offray ribbon, 3mm wide: 15 yds (14m) each of 250 red and 580 emerald
Anchor No. 5 pearl cotton, 5gm skeins: one each of 46 red and 228 green
Twilleys goldfingering: one ball each of 02 gold and 05 silver. As an alternative to the Twilleys gold fingering, Mez 'Diadem' could be used. Two 20m reels of each would be required

Preparation

1 Cut out 16 pieces each 14 bars square, eight pieces 13 bars square and four pieces 16 bars square.

Working the embroidery

2 Following the charts on page 68, work 2 of each of the following decorations in red and gold, and two of each in green and silver.

14 bars square (version 1)

3 Work a square of tent stitch in double pearl. Inside this, work a square of tent stitch in either the gold or silver metal thread. Fill in the centre with a Rhodes stitch in ribbon. This will be overcast to join with metal thread.

14 bars square (version 2)

4 Work a square of double cross stitch in double pearl and metal thread. Inside this, work a square of tent stitch in metal thread. Fill in with a satin stitch block in ribbon. This will be overcast to join with double pearl.

14 bars square (version 3)

5 Work a square of tent stitch in double pearl, then a triangle over 4 bars at each corner in double metal thread. Fill in the centres with triangles in ribbon. This will be overcast to join with metal thread.

14 bars square (version 4)

6 Work as version 3, reversing the metal thread and ribbon, overcasting together with double pearl.

13 bars square (version 1)

7 Work a square of tent stitch in metal thread. Fill in with a Norwich stitch in ribbon. This will be overcast to join with double pearl.

13 bars square (version 2)

8 Using metal thread, work a square of tent stitch round the outer edge, followed by a line over the centre bar in both directions. Fill in the 4 squares with satin stitch blocks in ribbon. This will be overcast to join with double pearl.

16 bars square

9 Trim off a square of 5 bars from each corner. Work 5 satin stitch blocks, leaving a bar space between. Work tent stitch round the centre block in metal thread. This will be overcast to join with metal thread.

Finishing

10 A loop may be made when the 2 sides of the decoration are being sewn together. Alternatively, after sewing the 2 squares together thread up a short length of ribbon and take it through the corner hole of the decoration. Knot the 2 ends firmly and trim close to the knot. Pull it through so that the knot lies close to the mesh.

11 Place 2 matching squares together, right sides outside, and overcast along 2 sides to join them. If making the loop as you stitch, wind the pearl cotton twice round 2 fingers, make a back stitch and complete the overcasting.

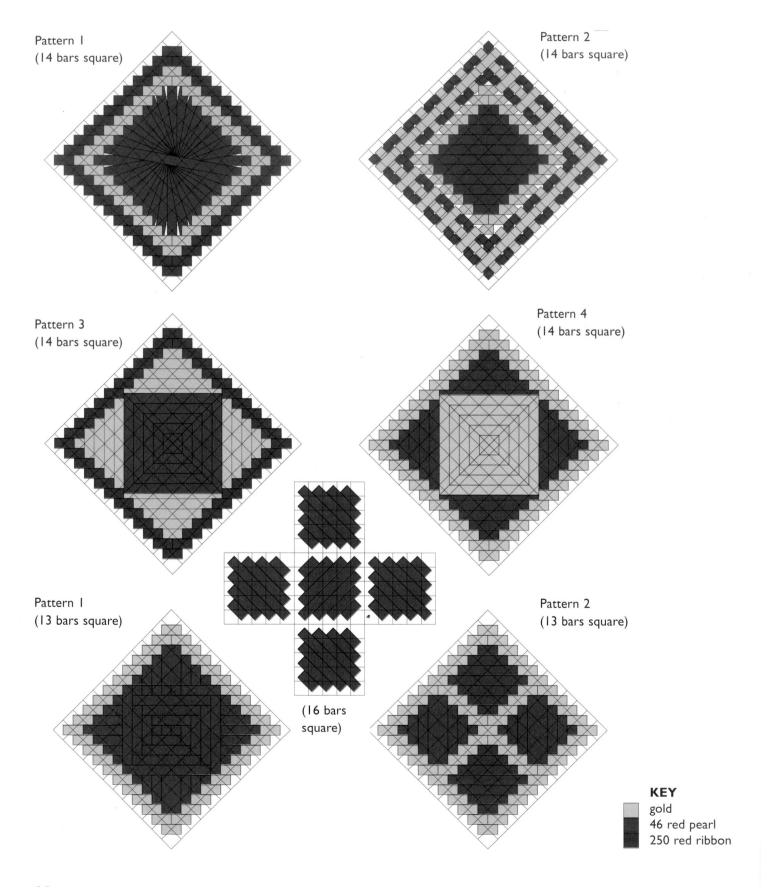

Pattern 1
(14 bars square)

Pattern 2
(14 bars square)

Pattern 3
(14 bars square)

Pattern 4
(14 bars square)

Pattern 1
(13 bars square)

(16 bars
square)

Pattern 2
(13 bars square)

KEY
gold
46 red pearl
250 red ribbon

Advent calendar

Children love the mystery of an advent calendar, and this is a particularly attractive way of using plastic canvas. The compartments behind the doors are quite roomy enough to take a choice of little gifts.

Materials

Plastic canvas 7 bars per 1in
(2.5cm): three sheets
18 x 12in (46 x 30cm) ultra
stiff and one sheet of standard
or super soft 18 x 12in
(46 x 30cm)
10 bars per 1in (2.5cm): three
sheets 13½ x 10½in
(34.5 x 26.5cm)
Paterna stranded wool, 8m
skeins: eleven 972 red, eight
681 green and one 260 white
Anchor stranded cotton, 8m
skeins: two 403 black and
three 228 Christmas green.
One each of 02 white, 46 red,
241 light green, 400 dark grey,
900 light grey, 393 grey/brown,

358 brown, 305 light yellow,
303 dark yellow, 271 pale pink,
118 lilac, 316 orange and 314
light orange
Twilleys goldfingering: one ball
02 gold and a small amount of
silver
1mm card: one piece
17½ x 11⅜in (44.5 x 29.5cm)
and one piece 17¼ x 11⅜in
(43.8 x 28.8cm)
Lightweight red or green
patterned fabric for covering
the back: two pieces each
19 x 13in (48 x 32cm)
2 small curtain rings
Velcro: 8in (20cm) with sticky
back
Latex or clear adhesive

Preparation

1 From 2 sheets of the ultra
stiff canvas, cut one bar
off one long and one short edge
for the back and front of the
calendar. From the third sheet,
cut 2 sides each 120 x 7 bars,
and two sides each 80 x 7 bars.

2 From the standard canvas,
cut 28 pieces each 50 x 6
bars for the inner box sides.
From the 10 count canvas, cut
48 doors each 24 x 18 bars and
2 central panels 47 x 75 bars.

KEY
Twilleys gold
46 red cotton
228 green cotton

KEY
Twilleys gold
681 green wool
972 red wool

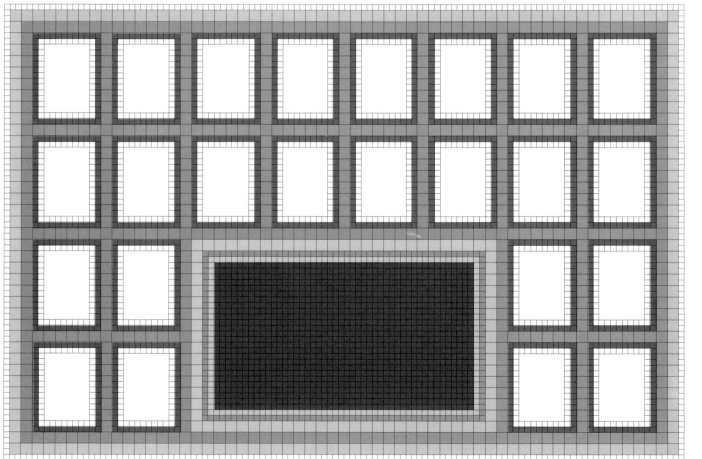

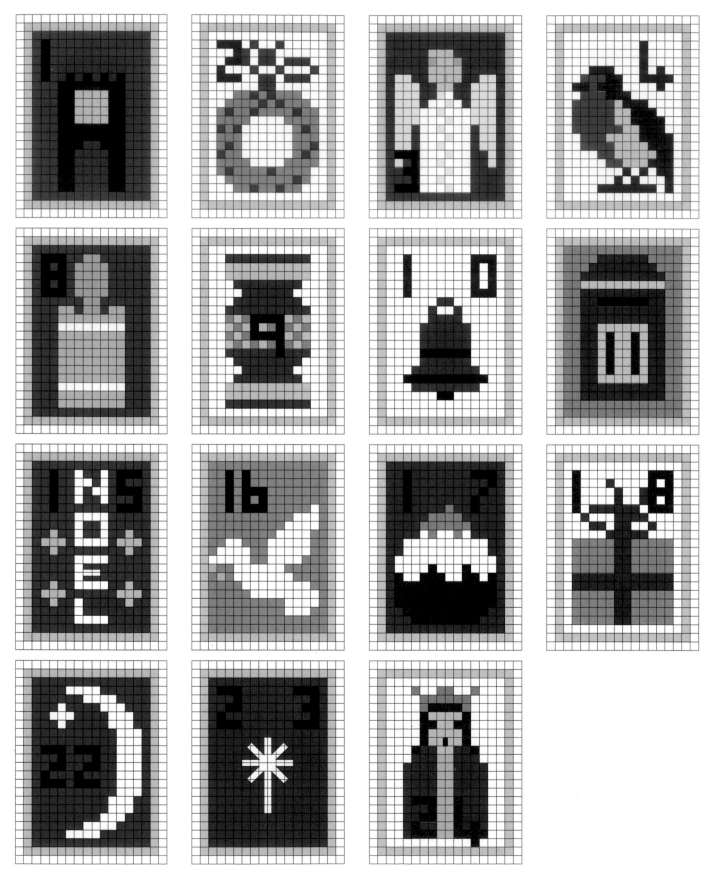

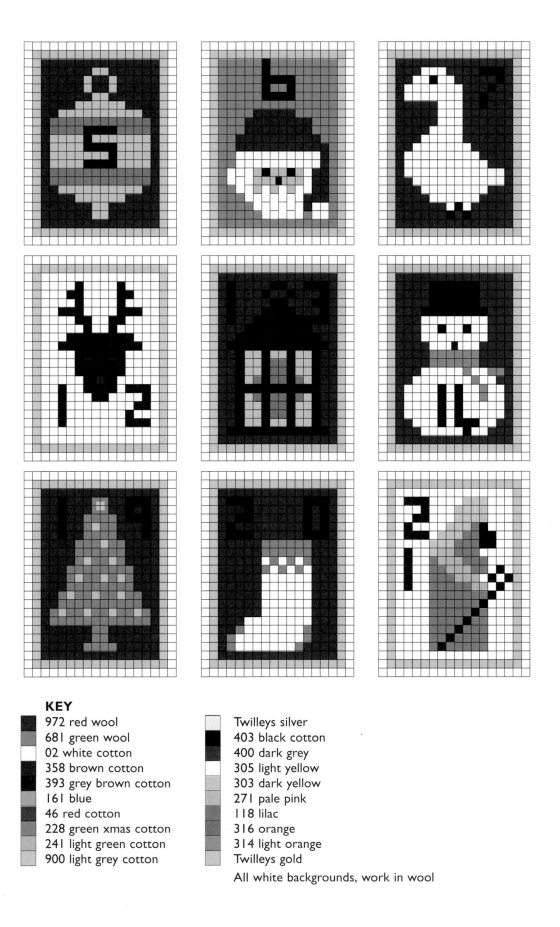

KEY

972 red wool
681 green wool
02 white cotton
358 brown cotton
393 grey brown cotton
161 blue
46 red cotton
228 green xmas cotton
241 light green cotton
900 light grey cotton

Twilleys silver
403 black cotton
400 dark grey
305 light yellow
303 dark yellow
271 pale pink
118 lilac
316 orange
314 light orange
Twilleys gold

All white backgrounds, work in wool

10 To prepare the doors, very carefully cut out the 24 uncovered areas of the main section, taking care to leave one bar beside the tent stitch. Trim off the butts and overcast all round the openings in red wool.

11 Place one embroidered door section over an inner door section, then overcast all round to join them, using 2 strands of red. Repeat for the other doors. Join the tree panel and its backing piece in the same way.

12 Using a single strand of red wool, slip stitch each box side section in place on the back of the panel behind a door opening, moulding it into an oval shape as you do so. To avoid fastening on and off, use a long length of wool. A couple of stitches at each corner of the doorway should be sufficient.

13 Run the needle through the stitches on the back to move from one position to the next. Make the remaining 4 uncovered box sides into rings and stitch behind the Christmas tree panel.

14 The doors may be placed at random or in numerical sequence. Lay each one in place, exactly over the opening, and overcast to join along the hinge edge, using a single strand of red wool. Take care to fasten on and off very securely. Slip stitch the tree panel in position

Working the embroidery

3 Use 2 strands of wool on the 7 count canvas and a single strand on the 10 count. Use the full 6 strands of the stranded cotton.

4 For the doors, work the 24 pictures in cross stitch using stranded cotton, following the chart on page 72, leaving the outer bar uncovered for joining later. The 24 pieces of canvas for the back of the doors need not be embroidered. Work the tree panel in the same way, using double yarn for the satin stitch border, following the chart on page 71.

5 For the front main section work in wool following the chart on page 71, leaving the door areas uncovered for cutting out later. Work the large squares in double cross stitch, and the small squares in tent stitch.

6 For the sides, work 2 lines of double cross stitch in green wool with a line of tent stitch in gold between, to cover the 4 sides.

7 For the 24 compartment sides, leaving the first and last 4 bars uncovered, cover the inner compartment sections with 2 lines of cross stitch over 2 bars. This does not completely cover the canvas, but is quite adequate.

8 Overlap the right edge over the left, matching up the bars, right side outside, and complete the cross stitch through both layers to form a ring.

9 Overcast round one edge, then turn through so that the right side of the cross stitch is inside the ring.

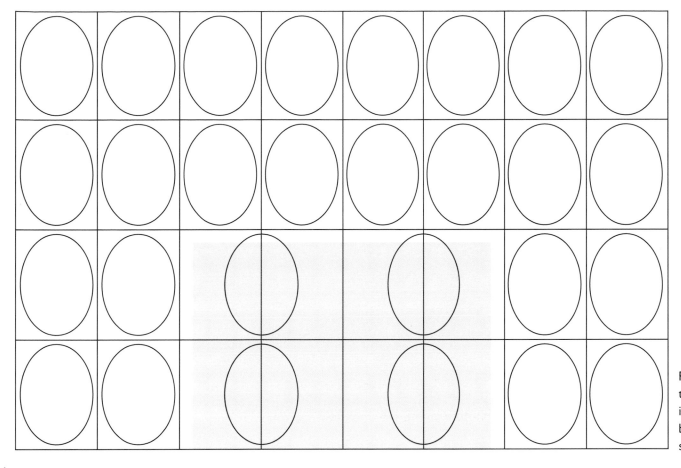

Placing the inner box sides

15 To make the back, place the fabric, right side down, with the card centrally over it. Fold the turnings over the card and stick in position. Slip stitch the larger piece to one side of the canvas for the back. Stitch the curtain rings 1in (2.5cm) from one long edge, about 5in (12.5cm) in from each corner.

16 To stitch up the main section, lay one embroidered side against the embroidered main section, right sides outside, edges matched up, and edge stitch to join. Repeat with the other 3 sides. Join the 4 corners to make a shallow box shape.

17 Place the box right side down and spread adhesive round the top edge of

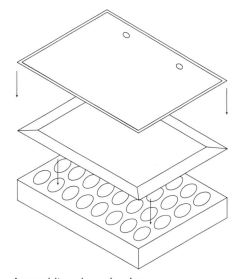

Assembling the calendar

the compartment sides. Carefully place the smaller covered card right side down centrally over this, taking care to position it correctly before allowing it to touch the glue. Press into position until bonded. Place the back in position, fabric side outside, and edge stitch to join it.

18 Cut a narrow section of velcro, about ¼in (6mm) wide, and stick it to the back of the opening edge of one door, positioning it in the centre. Repeat for the other doors.

> If preferred, you can substitute the words 'Merry Christmas' for the Christmas tree in the front panel.

Better Techniques

Good working methods have a marked effect on the standard of your work. For example, starting off with a knot on the front surface, which is cut off when it is reached, avoids the possibility of ends of yarns being brought to the surface as you stitch, spoiling the look of the embroidery.

Achieving the correct tension also enhances the finished work. If the tension is too loose the finished result will be rough and uneven, if too tight the canvas will show through and mar the appearance.

Before you start
In all the projects note the following:
• The amount of yarn needed for the different projects may vary slightly between individuals.
• In the charts, one square represents one stitch.
• One bar is left uncovered for joining or overcasting later.
• All figures in the size of canvas given refer to BARS not holes.
• Make each stitch in 2 moves, bringing the needle up and pulling the yarn through, taking it down and pulling it through.
• Try to keep the tension even by giving the yarn a slight tug as you make each stitch. When working on plastic canvas it is not always necessary to cover the canvas completely, as thinner yarns often give a more dainty textured appearance. However, you may prefer to work at a slightly looser tension than usual, allowing the yarn to puff out and give a good cover on the embroidery.

TYPES OF PLASTIC CANVAS
Sheets
Plastic canvas is available in pre-formed sheets, the largest is 22½ x 13½in (57 x 34cm). Sheets are easily joined together if you require a larger piece.

The bar count is in three sizes and some of the sheets come in stiff or soft variety. Not all of the types listed below are used in the projects, the information is given so that the designs may be adapted for other bar counts, if wished. The major producers are American, so measurements are usually in inches.

The mesh may differ slightly in bar count depending on the make, which can result in a slight difference in size of the finished item.

Circles
These are available in 9in (23cm), 6in (15cm), 4¼in (10.5cm) and 3in (7.5cm) sizes. All circles are approximately 7 count. They may vary slightly in size and construction. Most have radial holes to the centre, in others bars decrease in steps.

Cutting the canvas
Cut the canvas as required between the bars. Before beginning work, the butts should be trimmed off carefully, leaving a smooth edge, to prevent the yarn catching on them.

SUITABLE YARNS
Wools specially produced for embroidery are available from

TYPES OF SHEET PLASTIC CANVAS

SIZE	7 COUNT	10 COUNT	14 COUNT
8 x 11in (20 x 28cm)			Standard
10½ x 13½in (26.5 x 34.5cm)	Standard	Standard	
Bar count Darice	71 x 91	107 x 137	
Uniek	71 x 91	111 x 141	
12 x 18in (30 x 46cm)	Standard Ultra stiff Super soft		
Bar count	81 x 121		
13½ x 22½in (34 x 57cm)	Standard Ultra stiff		
Bar count	91 x 151		

several manufacturers, and what you are able to buy locally will depend on the particular brand stocked. Most are also available by mail order. A conversion chart for some of the available brands is given on page 80.

The advantages of using the specially produced wools are the high quality and resistance to fading and the large number of colours available. All yarns used should be washable.

Wool
The following are a selection of the most popular brands available.

Stranded or crewel: Paterna and Appletons. These wools have the advantage that the number of strands required may be selected for the project in hand. For example, as a rough guide, a single strand is needed on 14 count canvas, 2 strands on 10 count and 3 strands may be needed on 7 count.

Tapisserie: Anchor and DMC. These are single thicknesses, roughly equivalent in weight to a double knitting wool. They give a very smooth finish.

Pearl cotton
The most readily available are 5gm skeins. The length in each skein is approximately 20 yards or metres. They give an attractive variation in texture when used with wool.

Crochet cotton
Some crochet cotton is close to pearl cotton in appearance and makes an economical substitute. No. 3 or 5 would be needed. Colours are limited.

Ribbon
Two widths are suitable for working on plastic canvas, 3mm wide for 7 count and 1.5mm wide for 10 count.

Gold thread
The type used in this book is Twilleys goldfingering, which is available in 25gm balls, about 100 metres in length. It should be used doubled on 7 count canvas, singly on 10 count canvas. A good alternative would be Mez 'Diadem' which has 20 metres on a reel. This is a narrow ribbon type yarn and should be used singly on 7 count canvas.

JOINING THE CANVAS
Backing strip method for flat sections of mesh
Cut a piece of canvas 8 bars wide and the depth of the pieces which are to be joined together. Tack (baste) this to the right edge of the first section, underlapping it by 4 bars.

Work the embroidery on both sections, leaving the last 4 bars of the first section and the first 4 of the second, uncovered. Lap the left edge of the second section over the backing strip of the first, matching up 4 bars. Complete the embroidery through both layers at the join.

Backing strip method for a circular basket or box side
Cut the backing strip 8 bars wide by the depth of the section being embroidered. Tack (baste) this to the right short edge of the plastic canvas, underlapping it by 4 bars.

Leaving the first and last 4 bars uncovered, work the embroidery as required. Lap the left edge over the backing strip and complete the embroidery through both layers, so joining it into a ring. The same method is used when joining 2 sections.

Underlapping method
Leaving the first and last 4 bars uncovered, work the embroidery. Lap the right 4 bars of the main piece over the left 4 bars of the piece to be joined and then tack (baste) securely in place. Complete the embroidery through both layers. The same method is used for joining into a ring.

Joining a side section to a circular base
Place knots on the edge of the circle marking the 4 quarters, then place knots to mark the 4 quarters of the side section. Match up the knots when stitching together.

NEEDLES
A blunt-ended tapestry needle should be used. Size 20 is a good average size. Size 18 is larger and takes three strands of wool better. Size 16 is easier for children to thread.

THE STITCHES

Starting and finishing

Knot the end of the thread and take it through to the back of the work about 1in (2.5cm) forward from where you are intending to stitch. The stitches cover the thread on the back and the knot should be cut off when reached.

After the first row, the thread may be joined on by running through the back of previous stitching. Finish off by running the thread through the back of the last few stitches.

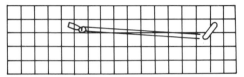

Tent stitch

Tent stitch passes over one intersection of the mesh and should be worked to give a long sloping stitch on the back, as this gives a good cover. Note that when stitching on a circle, the number of bars in a round reduces towards the centre. It is necessary to stitch twice into the same hole at intervals on the inner row, to keep the stitch sloping at the same angle.

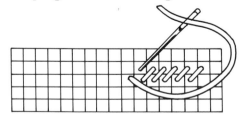

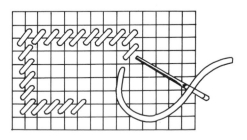

Small cross stitch

This stitch passes over one intersection of the mesh.

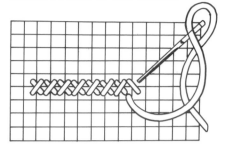

Large cross stitch

Large cross stitch is a cross worked over 2 intersections of the mesh.

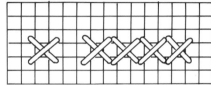

Double cross stitch

A cross stitch over 2 bars is worked first and then a straight cross stitch is worked over it to give a pleasing chunky stitch. The second cross may be in the same colour wool or in a contrasting colour, or in pearl cotton.

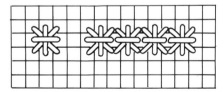

Long cross stitch

A long cross is worked across one bar and up over two. Lines may be worked diagonally across the canvas, in which case after the first stitch, the needle comes as follows for the start of the next stitch:

When going up the needle comes up in the middle of the previous stitch, and one bar to the right.

When going down the needle comes up one bar below the previous stitch, and one bar to the right.

For horizontal lines, the stitches are worked over alternate bars of the canvas for the first row. Stitches of subsequent rows fit between the first in a bricking effect. Small infilling stitches are needed along the edges.

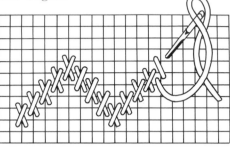

Rhodes stitch

This is usually a square stitch, but may also be rectangular, diamond shaped or circular – the method is the same. It is best worked over an even number of bars, from four upwards.

For a square stitch, start off with a long sloping stitch, coming up in the lower left corner and going down in the top right. Subsequent stitches come up one bar to the right and go down one bar to the left. On completion, the threads should be tied down with a small straight stitch across the centre. This may be omitted if the stitch is only 4 bars square.

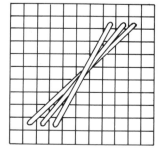

Norwich stitch

This is usually a square stitch, worked over an uneven number of bars. Although the numbering looks complicated, the stitch is actually very easy to work once the sequence is understood.

A large cross stitch is worked first, coming up at 1 and going down at 2, coming up at 3 and going down at 4. After this, it will be seen that the needle always comes up on the same side of the square as it went down, and then crosses over and goes down on the adjacent side.

If worked correctly, there will be long straight stitches round the edge of the square on the back of the work. Following the diagram, you will see that 6 and 7 are on the same side, as are 8 and 9, 10 and 11 and so on, round the square.

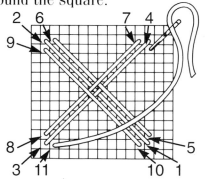

Satin stitch lines

Sloping stitches are worked over 2 bars. As a filling stitch, this looks decorative if adjacent lines slope in alternate directions.

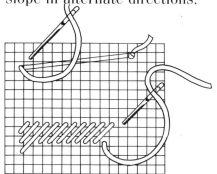

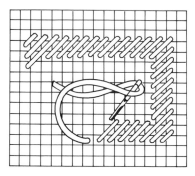

Satin stitch squares

These may be either square or rectangular, according to the shape to be filled.

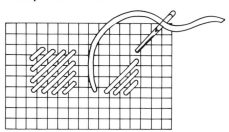

Edge stitch

This stitch is used for joining sections together, or for covering an edge. It has an interesting plaited effect, which shows best if worked from the wrong side. Work at a tight tension.

Although it may look complicated, the stitch is actually just 2 movements – forward three and back two, repeated. Extra stitches are needed at the beginning and end to fill in properly.

Following the diagram, bring the needle up in the first hole, take it over the edge and come out at 2, two bars forward. Take it back over the edge and bring it out two bars back, in the first hole again. *Take it over the edge, and out three bars forward. Take it over the edge and out two bars back. Repeat from * along the edge until the needle comes up in the last hole. Take it back over the edge and out one bar

back, and bring it up in the last hole again. Fasten off securely. When turning a corner, work 3 stitches into the corner hole, and continue along the next side.

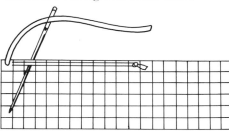

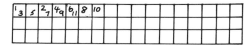

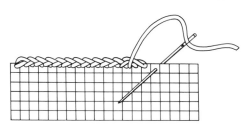

Overcasting

This stitch may need a thicker yarn than has been used in the embroidery. For example, 3 strands of Paterna give a good cover on 7 count canvas and 2 strands on 10 count.

Bring the needle up in the first hole, take it over the edge and out again in the first hole. This ensures that there is no gap at the beginning. Take it over the edge and bring it up again in the second hole. Continue like this along the edge, bringing the needle through from the back each time.

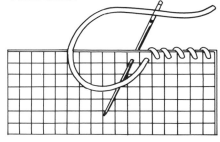

CONVERSION CHART

Tapestry wool, pearl and stranded cotton substitution chart (same strand numbers apply to both stranded and pearl cottons).

Anchor	DMC	Anchor	DMC	Anchor	DMC	Anchor	DMC
2	neige	168	807	316	740	891	676
8	353	203	954	369	435	942	738
9	352	214	368	372	738	977	334
10	351	216	367	375	420	8006	ecru
19	347	265	989	386	746	8396	7105
74	605	293	727	398	415	8436	7135
75	3354	295	726	400	317	8438	7436
77	3350	306	783	403	310	8626	7283
108	211	307	783	850	926	8964	7952
118	793	308	782	874	834	9800	7309
167	3766	314	741	885	3047		

Twilleys metallic thread   Kreinik thread

ACKNOWLEDGEMENTS

I would like to thank my husband for his patient help and encouragement in the preparation of this book. He has helped me master the word processor, patiently edited the script and spent many a happy and peaceful evening working some of the samples.

I thank Hilary Harrison for the design of the sampler. For help with the embroidery, sincere and grateful thanks to Hilary Harrison, Pauline Newlands, Wendy Newlands and Nancy Perrin.

STOCKISTS AND SUPPLIERS

U.K.

Meg Evans, 29 New Road, Welwyn, Herts AL6 0AQ
Mail order for most items listed in the projects.

Shades at Mace and Nairn, 89 Crane Street, Salisbury, Wiltshire SP1 2PY
Mail order for a very wide range of supplies.

For a list of countrywide shops write to the following:
Coats Crafts UK, McMullen Road, Darlington, Co Durham, DL1 1YQ

DMC Creative World, Pullman Road, Wigston, Leicestershire LE8 2DY

For list of Paterna stockists:
The Craft Collection, PO Box 1, Ossett, West Yorkshire WF5 9SA

Ribbons:
C M Offray & Son Ltd, Fir Tree Place, Church Road, Ashford, Middlesex TW15 2PH

Australia

Coats Patons Crafts, 89-91 Peters Avenue, Mulgrave, Victoria 3170

DMC Needlecraft Pty Ltd, 57-66 Carrington Road, Marrickville, NSW 2204
PO Box 317 Earlswood, NSW 2206

U.S.A.

Coats & Clark Inc, 30 Patewood Drive, Suite 351, Grenville, sc 29615

The DMC Corporation Port Kearny, Building 10, South Kearny, NJ07032

Mail order suppliers in U.S.A.:
Schrocks Crafts, 1527 East Amherst Road, Massillon, Ohio 44646

Needlecraft Shop, 103 North Pearl Street, Big Sandy, Texas 75755

Sunshine Crafts, 1280 North Missouri Avenue, Largo, Florida 34640

C M Offray & Son Inc, Route 24, PO Box 601, Chester, New Jersey 07930 0601